REVISITING
U.S. TRADE POLICY

REVISITING
U.S. TRADE POLICY

Decisions in Perspective

edited by

Alfred E. Eckes, Jr.

OHIO UNIVERSITY PRESS
ATHENS

Ohio University Press, Athens, Ohio 45701

Printed in the United States of America

Ohio University Press books are printed on acid-free paper ∞

04 03 02 01 00 5 4 3 2 1

Library of Congress Cataloging-in-Publication Data

Revisiting U.S. Trade Policy: decisions in perspective/
edited by Alfred E. Eckes, Jr.
p. cm.
Includes bibliographical references.
ISBN 0-8214-1323-6 (cloth : alk. paper)
1. United States—Commercial policy—History—20th century
2. General Agreement on Tariffs and Trade (Organization)
3. Kennedy Round (1964-1967 : Geneva, Switzerland)
4. Tokyo Round (1973-1979)
I. Title: Revisiting US Trade Policy.
II. Title: Revisiting United States Trade Policy.
III. Eckes, Alfred E., 1942-

HF1455 .R427 2000
382'.3'0973—dc21

99-086404

CONTENTS

PREFACE

THIS ORAL HISTORY OFFERS an unusual retrospective assessment of late-twentieth-century U.S. trade policy that should prove valuable to students and scholars, and relevant to the needs of government policymakers, legislators, and other officials. In 1997 and 1998 the editor, on behalf of the U.S. International Trade Commission (ITC) Historical Society, invited thirty-five former policymakers and negotiators to participate in a series of roundtable discussions relating to some of the most significant chapters in the history of post–World War II American trade. The topics selected were the General Agreement on Tariffs and Trade (GATT), which is the predecessor to the World Trade Organization (WTO), and the Kennedy and Tokyo Rounds of multilateral trade negotiations, two of the most significant held under GATT auspices. Several scholars, who had done extensive archival research or interviews with trade officials, also were invited to ask questions and help guide the colloquies.

What was the rationale for undertaking this project? Those who have worked with trade policy know that most disputes have a lengthy and bitter past and frequently a contentious future. The United States and Canada, for example, have battled over lumber, fish, wheat, and potatoes for more than a century. A series of agricultural disputes—involving such things as chickens, wine, butter, and beef—have long disrupted trade relations with European countries. For much of the last half century the U.S. steel industry has periodically invoked trade remedy laws to address surges in dumped and subsidized steel imports. In short, in trade policy—and perhaps in many other government policy areas as well—the past is often both present and prologue. Decision makers unfamiliar with earlier disputes, and how policymakers sought to resolve them, often seem condemned to repeat the past. The same also may occur in trade negotiations. Former Commerce Department negotiator Clyde Prestowitz has complained that U.S. trade officials are sometimes so blind to previous bargains that they buy the same horse again from more experienced foreign negotiators.[1]

It is a regrettable reality of the process of government that officials seldom have the opportunity to revisit critical decisions in the past and to assess the significance of their actions after considerable time has elapsed. This seems particularly true in the trade area. Part of the explanation relates to the high turnover of presidential appointees, who average perhaps eighteen months in office before moving to new opportunities. The U.S. system of government assigns a premium to periodic rotation in office; whereas many foreign governments spend years training successive generations of decision makers. Another part of the explanation relates to the optimistic American style and to the confidence of officeholders that careful study of present circumstances will lead to intelligent solutions. Often policymakers confront difficult decisions without knowledge of the relevant historical record. There is no central repository of documents pertaining to past trade negotiations and administrative decisions. Some files have been deposited in presidential libraries, others removed when appointees left office, and others have been transferred to the National Archives. Thus, each generation faces the future with only limited understanding of previous initiatives—and much of that information obtained from a few senior-level civil servants, such as William T. Hart, the former director of government liaison at the ITC, whose memory and experience spanned nearly a half century of negotiations.

While a few participants in the Kennedy Round, such as John Evans and Ernest Preeg, have written contemporary accounts of interest to practitioners, the writing of trade history is usually left to academic historians and political scientists.[2] These scholars face many obstacles. For one thing, they must struggle to gain access to classified documents and to cope with cumbersome declassification rules. Because trade policy involves a complex interagency process, the process of declassifying documents can prove quite time consuming. Along with the usual difficulties of locating relevant contemporary media accounts and of gaining access to key participants, academics frequently face another burden. They may lack a sophisticated understanding of the trade policy process unless they have firsthand experience in government. Consequently their interpretations, which are intended for other scholars and students, frequently offer little concrete guidance to policymakers eager to learn how their predecessors organized previous negotiations or addressed some of the arcane problems—such as pertain to individual industries like steel, textiles, and agriculture. The burning questions that arouse academic interest seldom are the same ones that trouble practitioners.

Sylvia K. Kraemer of the National Aeronautics and Space Administration, who holds a Ph.D. in history, has written about the gap between academic writings and government needs. She says that "current historical writing has too little to say of compelling value to those who do the very hard work of finding politically viable solutions to the large public questions of our day, day in and day out." She argues that "experience in policy making can offer as much to the continuing education of a historian as the knowledge of history can enlighten the policy-maker."[3] I agree.

Recognizing the need for a more accessible history to guide policymakers and legislators, as well as the interested public, the U.S. International Trade Commission Historical Society (ITCHS) began a program of oral histories in 1996, which includes this series on major trade policy decisions. In selecting discussants, we sought both the participation of principals and of supporting staff. We strove to include representatives of the major agencies involved in the trade policy process. We also sought participation from Congress, but several of the invitees had scheduling conflicts, or could not participate for other reasons. Lacking the resources to reimburse travel expenses, we did not actively seek foreign participation—thinking that initially it was important to hear from a representative group of U.S. negotiators and policymakers. The resulting document is somewhat unidimensional. It is rich on the U.S. executive branch's interpretation of events but thin on congressional perspectives and foreign perceptions.

In preparation for the sessions the editor sent participants a list of proposed discussion topics together with a selection of declassified documents and newspaper clippings. The latter, intended to help refresh memories, were obtained from holdings of the John F. Kennedy, Lyndon B. Johnson, and Jimmy Carter presidential libraries, as well as from on-line newspaper sources. Sitting as a panel—with a public audience—these specialists then worked their way through the negotiations, discussing relevant documents and events, and offering their own retrospective assessments of their successes and failures. Professor Eckes, president of the ITCHS in 1997, moderated the discussions with the assistance of William T. Hart, the organization's vice president.

Our experiences may have broader relevance for scholars and government officials interested in the history of some public policy area or institution. One lesson is that a big budget is not essential for a project of this kind. The ITC Historical Society lacked resources to pay participants honoraria or to reimburse travel and expenses. Several small grants, including one from the Jimmy Carter Presidential Library, did help pay for essential expenses, such as tapes and refreshments for the participants. While the ITCHS had a shoestring budget, it did have certain intangible assets. Our members had an extensive network of personal contacts, and they shared an enthusiasm for undertaking a project of some historical significance.

The ITC Historical Society is a private nonprofit charitable and educational association incorporated in 1995. Its purposes are to encourage "the study of the history of the United States Tariff Commission and its successor agency, the United States International Trade Commission"; and "to increase the awareness of the trade laws and policies of the United States." Bruce Clubb, a former member of the U.S. Tariff Commission and a partner in the law firm of Baker and McKenzie, proposed the idea of a historical association to study the Tariff Commission. His model was the Supreme Court Historical Society, which brings together scholars and practitioners to study the court. A steering committee composed of Clubb, Bill Alberger, Alfred Eckes, Bill Leonard, Ken Mason, David B. Rohr, and Paula Stern met on April 7, 1995, and proposed that the new historical organization also seek to promote a broader understanding of the history of American trade policy. Clubb consented to serve as the first president of the new organization, and he was succeeded by David B. Rohr (1996), Alfred Eckes (1997), Lynn M. Bragg (1998), and Donald Dinan (1999). Kenneth Mason, once the secretary of the ITC, is secretary of the historical society. Lorin Goodrich, formerly the ITC's director of administration, is treasurer.

A number of individuals and organizations merit special thanks for assisting with this unique oral history project. In particular, I would like to express appreciation to the thirty-five policymakers and scholars who participated in these discussions. They all gave generously of their time and experiences. Despite busy professional and personal schedules, they diligently reviewed briefing materials and carefully prepared for the sessions. To join the discussions, some of them even traveled long distances at considerable personal expense.

When this series was first proposed, some wondered if it was too ambitious. They questioned whether members of the group—some of whom had not seen one another for thirty years and had pursued later career paths unrelated to trade—would consent to participate, or be able to recall anything of significance twenty-five or thirty years after the completion of negotiations. As it turned out, these concerns were misplaced. Almost all of the invitees agreed to participate. Initially, a few of the group did express some hesitation, thinking they might have forgotten too much to be helpful to this historical inquiry. But, as often happens, the group experience inspired and stimulated individuals. Latent memories revived. Soon enthusiastic discussants were recalling stories and perspectives they had not contemplated for many years. On a few occasions, the group discussion even revived old policy disputes and institutional conflicts.

The editor helped organize the programs, select the panelists, and moderate the sessions included in the present volume. In these activities I benefited greatly from the experience and knowledge of William T. Hart, a forty-eight-year veteran of the trade negotiating process, and the vice president of the ITC

Historical Society. I would also like to thank William Kelly, Ken Mason, Bernard Norwood, and John Rehm for their many suggestions on how to organize and implement the programs. But, the editor, who personally transcribed tapes from the discussion sessions, accepts responsibility for any editorial mistakes that may inadvertently have occurred in preparing the volume for publication.

Among the officers and members of the ITC Historical Society, Bill Hart, Ken Mason, Lorin Goodrich, Louise Burghart, and Elli Nesbitt deserve special recognition. They were especially helpful in facilitating conference arrangements.

This project could not have been completed without assistance from members and staff of the U.S. International Trade Commission. I would particularly like to thank Chairman Lynn M. Bragg, who supported these efforts enthusiastically, and served as the fourth president of the ITC Historical Society, as well as Tyrone Coward and William Bishop, who aided with technical arrangements.

Among the presidential libraries, the Jimmy Carter Presidential Library was most helpful and supportive. It provided a small grant that helped cover the costs of the conference on the Tokyo Round, and Don Schewe, the director of the Carter library, facilitated access to declassified materials.

Finally, we owe thanks to Ohio University and to the Ohio University Press for supporting this oral history project and for publishing the present volume.

ABBREVIATIONS

AFL-CIO—American Federation of Labor-Congress of Industrial Organizations
APEC—Asia-Pacific Economic Cooperation
ASP—American selling price
BIS—Bank for International Settlements
CAP—common agricultural policy
CP-18—Consultative Group of Eighteen Contracting Parties
CXT—common external tariff
DG-1—Directorate-General I (External Relations)
DISC—Domestic International Sales Corporation
EC—European Community
ECAT—Emergency Committee for American Trade
EEC—European Economic Community
EFTA—European Free Trade Association
EU—European Union
GATT—General Agreement on Tariffs and Trade
GDP—Gross Domestic Product
G-7—Group of Seven [industrialized nations]
ILO—International Labor Organization
IMF—International Monetary Fund
INR—initial negotiating right
ISAC—industry sector advisory committee
ITC—U.S. International Trade Commission
ITCHS—U.S. International Trade Commission Historical Society
ITO—International Trade Organization [1948]
LDC—less developed country
MFN—most favored nation
MTN—multilateral trade negotiations
NAFTA—North American Free Trade Agreement
NTB—nontariff barrier

NTT—Nippon Telephone and Telegraph
OECD—Organization for Economic Cooperation and Development
OTC—Organization for Trade Cooperation
STR—U.S. Special Representative for Trade Negotiations [October 1962 to January 1980]
TPC—Trade Policy Committee
TPRG—Trade Policy Review Group
TPSC—Trade Policy Staff Committee
TRIPS—trade-related aspects of intellectual property rights
TSUS—Tariff Schedules of the United States
UAW—United Auto Workers
UNCTAD—United Nations Conference on Trade and Development
USDA—U.S. Department of Agriculture
USTR—U.S. Trade Representative [January 1980 to present]
WTO—World Trade Organization [est. 1995]

BIOGRAPHICAL SKETCHES

Francis M. Bator, a Hungarian-born economist, served as deputy assistant for national security affairs to President Lyndon Johnson (1965-67). Upon leaving government he became a professor of political economy at the John F. Kennedy School of Government, Harvard University.

Herbert Blackman, a government economist with experience in the Treasury, War Production Board, Commerce, and Labor Departments, was administrator of the bureau of international labor affairs in the Department of Labor during the Kennedy Round. Subsequently, he served that department as associate deputy undersecretary for international affairs.

Ambassador *W. Michael Blumenthal,* a German-born economist, served in the State Department and then as deputy special trade representative in Geneva (1963-67). Upon leaving government he became president of Bendix Corp., and later secretary of the treasury (1977-79).

I. M. Destler, a political scientist, teaches at the University of Maryland and is a visiting fellow at the Institute for International Economics. Among his many publications on trade is *American Trade Politics: System under Stress* (1986).

Steve Dryden, a journalist, has covered trade policy for the *International Herald Tribune,* the *Washington Post,* and *Bloomberg Financial News.* He is the author of *Trade Warriors: USTR and the American Crusade for Free Trade* (1995).

Alfred E. Eckes is a research professor in contemporary history at Ohio University and president of the International Trade and Finance Association. He served as commissioner (and chairman) of the U.S. International Trade Commission (1981-90). He is the author of *Opening America's Market: U.S. Foreign Trade Policy since 1776* (1995).

Lawrence Fox held a number of positions in the Department of Commerce from 1949 to 1975. During the early phase of the Tokyo Round he was deputy assistant secretary of commerce for international economic policy; and subsequently he was vice president for international economic affairs of the National Association of Manufacturers.

Theodore R. Gates, an international economist with the National Industrial Conference Board (1950-63) became chief economist and then assistant special trade representative (1963-73).

John D. Greenwald, the son of Joseph A. Greenwald, served as deputy general counsel in the office of the U.S. Trade Representative (1974-80). Subsequently, he was deputy assistant secretary of commerce for import administration (1980-81).

Joseph A. Greenwald was deputy assistant secretary for international trade policy in the State Department during the Kennedy Round. Subsequently, he served as ambassador to the Organization for Economic Cooperation and Development (1969-72).

William T. Hart, vice president of the ITC Historical Society, served as director of executive liaison for the U.S. Tariff Commission and subsequently the U.S. International Trade Commission. In that capacity he participated in international trade negotiations, and interagency policy work, over a period of government service extending from 1948 to 1996.

Dale Hathaway, a former chairman of the agricultural economics department at Michigan State University, was undersecretary of agriculture for international affairs and commodity programs in the Carter administration. Later he served as executive director of the National Center for Food and Agricultural Policy.

Irwin R. Hedges held a variety of government positions in agriculture and development beginning in 1935. He joined the staff of the Special Trade Representative (STR) in 1963 to specialize in agricultural issues. Subsequently he became the first coordinator of Food for Peace, a federal program in the Agency for International Development delivering surplus American food to needy nations.

Gary Hufbauer was deputy assistant secretary of the treasury for international trade and investment policy (1977-80). A lawyer and economist, he is a senior fellow with the Institute for International Economics in Washington, D.C.

Jules Katz worked in the State Department from 1950 to 1979, serving as assistant secretary of state for economic and business affairs (1976–79). During the Bush administration he was deputy U.S. trade representative.

William B. Kelly began his government career in the State Department and served in the Commerce Department. He was assigned to permanent delegation in Geneva. Kelly joined the office of STR after the Kennedy Round and became chairman of the interagency Trade Policy Committee (TPC), chairing it during the Tokyo Round. From 1980 to 1987 he was a deputy director general of GATT.

Ambassador *Jeffrey Lang* was appointed deputy U.S. trade representative in 1995. A lawyer, he served as trade counsel to the Senate Finance Committee from 1979 to 1990, working closely with Senators Russell Long (D-La.) and Lloyd Bentsen (D-Tex.).

James H. Lewis, a foreign service officer, joined the trade agreements division of the State Department in 1936 and subsequently participated in GATT negotiations in Annecy, Torquay, and Geneva. During the Kennedy Round he was deputy head of the U.S. delegation.

Harald Malmgren, an economist, served as an assistant U.S. trade representative during the Kennedy Round and then as ambassador and deputy U.S. special trade representative (1972–75). He subsequently established a trade consulting firm.

Richard Matthiessen began working at the Department of Commerce in 1955 and gained a reputation as an authority on the GATT. He moved to USTR and spent several years in USTR's Geneva office during the 1980s handling the day-to-day issues at GATT.

Ambassador *Alonzo McDonald,* managing director of McKinsey and Company, became deputy special trade representative (Geneva) in charge of the U.S. delegation. Subsequently, he served as an assistant to President Carter and White House staff director (1979–81). He later became president of the Bendix Corporation and chairman of the Avenir Group.

Robert L. McNeill served as deputy assistant secretary of commerce for trade policy (1963–67) and then executive vice chairman of the Emergency Committee for American Trade (ECAT).

Douglas Newkirk, during the Tokyo Round, was responsible for negotiations that resulted in the government procurement code. He joined USTR after the Tokyo Round to handle operations of the government procurement code and related matters. For several years before his recent retirement Doug was the assistant USTR for GATT Affairs.

Bernard Norwood, an economist and a foreign service officer, chaired the trade staff committee in the office of the Special Trade Representative (1963–67). Subsequently, he worked for the board of governors of the Federal Reserve System and Nathan Associates (1975–94).

Gardner Patterson, a prominent international economist and professor of economics at Princeton University, was deputy director general of GATT during the Kennedy Round. He retired from GATT in 1981.

Amy Porges is an international lawyer and current member of the USTR staff. She has been involved with GATT matters over much of the last twenty years, and has a keen interest in trade history. She serves as senior counsel for dispute settlement.

Margaret Potter-Leddy began working on trade policy when she entered the State Department in 1938. Except during World War II, she remained involved with trade matters, and became chief of the trade agreements branch. Subsequently, she joined the U.S. Mission in Geneva to handle GATT matters. After retiring from the State Department in 1962, she worked another eight years for the GATT secretariat.

Ernest Preeg, an economist, served in the foreign service, U.S. Department of State (1963–88). From 1981 to 1983 he was U.S. ambassador to Haiti. During the Kennedy Round he was economist to the U.S. delegation.

John B. Rehm, a State Department lawyer, became general counsel in the office of the Special Trade Representative (1963–69). Upon leaving government in 1969, he practiced international trade law in Washington, D.C.

Ambassador *William M. Roth,* a businessman with experience in energy, insurance, and shipping, was deputy special trade representative (1963–66). He succeeded Gov. Christian Herter as special trade representative with the rank of ambassador (1967–69).

Howard Samuel, a labor union official with the Amalgamated Clothing and Textile Workers, was deputy undersecretary of labor during the Tokyo Round. Subsequently, he served as president of the industrial union department, AFL-CIO.

John A. Schnittker, an agricultural economist from Kansas, served as undersecretary of agriculture from 1965 to 1969. Subsequently, he worked as an agricultural consultant with Schnittker Associates.

Ambassador *Michael Smith* joined the State Department in 1958 and became the first textile negotiator in the Office of the Special Trade Representative in 1977. He served in Geneva as deputy USTR from 1979 to 1983, and then returned to Washington, D.C., where he continued as deputy USTR until 1988. In that position he frequently chaired the Trade Policy Review Group (TPRG).

Ambassador *Robert S. Strauss,* a partner in the law firm of Akin, Gump, Strauss, Hauer, and Feld, served as chairman of the Democratic National Committee (1972–77), and then became special trade representative (1977–79). He chaired President Carter's reelection campaign and served as U.S. ambassador to Russia (1991–93).

S. Bruce Wilson held a number of positions in the Office of the STR/USTR (1975–91) and then became Democratic trade counsel to the House Ways and Means Committee. He is a partner in the law firm of Akin, Gump, Strauss, Hauer, and Feld.

Ambassador *Alan William Wolff,* a lawyer who became general counsel of STR, served as deputy special trade representative (1977–79). He is managing partner of Dewey, Ballantine, in Washington, D.C.

Thomas Zeiler, a historian who teaches at the University of Colorado, Boulder, is author of *American Trade and Power in the 1960s* (1992), a history of the Kennedy Round, and *Free Trade, Free World: The Advent of GATT* (1999).

✧ CHAPTER ONE

Introduction

IN THIS ORAL HISTORY a distinguished group of thirty-five former trade decision makers from the executive branch revisit some of the highlights of America's trade liberalization program in the years after World War II. They evaluate U.S. participation in the General Agreement on Tariffs and Trade (GATT), and analyze the Kennedy and Tokyo rounds of multilateral trade negotiations. Generally, the officials assess these initiatives positively, but they are not uncritical.

Underlying these discussions is the belief that history matters. Twentieth-century trade history is about the flowering of a big concept—an open international economy with rules for participants—and the recurrence of country- and product-specific disputes. Details of the latter are often vital to the success of major trade negotiations. After hearing how important chicken parts were to the Kennedy Round, Deputy USTR Jeff Lang noted that he too had recently negotiated on chickens. "Details don't change in trade. Trade negotiations thrive on attention to detail." To be persuasive with negotiating partners, he said, "you must have people who are prepared to master detail" (p. 84).[1]

While it is not possible to summarize the full discussion in the space available, much of it has continuing relevance in myriad ways for policymakers and for scholars seeking to understand better America's trade liberalization program and the phenomenal growth of globalization. Most readers will want to review the full transcripts and consult the detailed index.

Chapter 2 focuses on GATT, the provisional organization that endured for nearly a half century until establishment of the World Trade Organization in 1995 and hosted eight rounds of multilateral negotiations. How did those most involved with GATT evaluate this experience? While it lacked the international standing and powers of the International Trade Organization (ITO) proposed in 1948, GATT proved important to the postwar world. Doug Newkirk notes that it "provided a framework, a sense of security, and transparency for a large portion of world trade, particularly among developed countries" (p. 42).

Did GATT facilitate what would have happened anyway? Discussants Michael B. Smith and William Kelly reject that argument. While there was an inevitability to trade expansion once the world recovered from World War II, trade liberalization and the opening of markets were not inevitable. Those who defend GATT's achievements, such as Kelly, make the point that GATT produced a more efficient allocation of world resources. "Suppose none of these rounds had happened. . . . I think we would have such a misallocation of resources that we could not possibly have the kind of growth and the dynamic economy that we have today. So the real benefits of the GATT process are the efficiencies in U.S. and foreign production that have led to higher standards of living and growth" (p. 34).

Ironically, GATT began inauspiciously. The U.S. plan for an ITO, negotiated at the Havana Conference in 1948, failed to pass muster with Congress. GATT, which was a provisional arrangement pending establishment of the ITO, endured because the U.S. executive branch chose to treat it as a contractual agreement. One trade policy veteran, Margaret Potter-Leddy, recalls how GATT was "drafted in a very clever way so that there was a structure there even though it was not evident, and it was not evident to Congress, in particular!" The trick was to capitalize the phrase "Contracting Parties," to thus establish an organization and a contractual relationship (p. 23). Rather than risk a congressional vote on GATT, says Smith, "one U.S. administration after another hid behind the concept of Contracting Parties, saying we had a legal obligation. . . . In fact, it was questionable whether we really did have an obligation" (p. 38).

Did overzealous bureaucrats thus succeed in imposing GATT on less focused political leaders? Smith rejects that view, arguing that because ultimately everything stops at the White House, GATT's endurance is attributable to a national political will expressed informally by a series of presidents and key members of Congress, like House Ways and Means Chairman Wilbur Mills (pp. 38–39).

The GATT panelists also debated the significance of several momentous policy decisions. One was the American decision not to join the ITO in 1948 or 1949. Might a successful launching of ITO in the years after World War II have made a significant difference to the world trading system? Some participants thought the ITO experiment would have worked poorly. Kelly, a former deputy director general of GATT, said that after World War II nations were not ready for provisions relating to investments, services, and some of the other things in the present WTO. Nations in Europe and Asia were devastated and unable to implement trade liberalization obligations. Any attempt to impose mandatory dispute resolution or to address problems of services and investments at that stage might have broken down the system. Amy Porges, who presently is responsible for dispute settlement work at USTR, suggests that there was a vast gap between the aspirations of the founders of the GATT system and the readiness of governments to accept obligations. "We are beginning to catch up, but it really has taken fifty years" (p. 24).

Another turning point was the Soviet decision to decline GATT membership. Michael Smith says this "was an unknown blessing at the time, much as their decision to walk out of the United Nations Security Council was at the time of the Korean War." Participants think a Soviet decision to join GATT likely would have politicized the trade liberalization, and made GATT ineffective. But, as a result of the Soviet decision, GATT became an "arrow in the Western world's quiver, much like the Marshall Plan became" (pp. 21–22).

Is GATT dead? Yes and no, the participants said. Yes, in the sense that the Uruguay Round agreement formally killed GATT so as to end waivers and special privileges and to force every nation to adhere to the WTO on identical terms. No, in the sense that the WTO incorporates the trade-liberalizing spirit of GATT and extends it to new areas such as services.

A different group of former officials discussed and evaluated the Kennedy Round, the sixth round of multilateral negotiations. Chapter 3 contains an edited version of that transcript. The Kennedy Round, involving some forty countries, concluded in May 1967. President Lyndon Johnson said it produced the "most successful multilateral agreement on tariff reduction ever negotiated."[2] The agreement brought average tariff cuts of 36 to 39 percent among participating industrial countries, and addressed such nontariff issues as dumping. But there was little progress in agriculture, and forty-one developing countries refused to participate. Another seventeen countries negotiated under special arrangements that did not require reciprocity. These included some countries with large potential markets, such as Brazil, India, Indonesia, and Pakistan.

In revisiting these events, the panelists emphasized the crucial importance of individuals and leadership. Two persons in particular made the Kennedy Round possible: Undersecretary of State George Ball, who found a compelling rationale for trade liberalization—the challenge of the European Community—and thus revived a faltering trade liberalization program, and House Ways and Means Chairman Wilbur Mills. A supporter of trade liberalization, Mills found a way to make a new mandate of negotiating authority palatable to a skeptical Congress. He did so by reorganizing the bureaucracy and shifting trade away from the State Department to the Special Trade Representative in the White House.

Also crucial to the success of the Kennedy Round negotiations, the participants say, was strong U.S. leadership. Washington pushed a divided Europe, as well as a reluctant Japan and Canada, to the bargaining table. These were the real players in trade negotiations of the 1960s. Developing countries wanted merely to obtain concessions without providing reciprocity. "What will you give us? We need it, but of course we can't pay," Michael Blumenthal recalled them as thinking (p. 63). John Rehm cites an example of President Johnson's leadership skills when, at a cabinet meeting in 1967, he asked officials in his own inimitable style to look ahead fifty years and indicate whether it would be in the U.S. interest to accept the proposed deal. Rehm said that he sat there thinking, "That's what a president of the United States should do" (p. 111).

As they had in prior GATT negotiations, many in the U.S. agricultural community had high hopes for obtaining improved access to European markets, but these hopes could not be fulfilled. As Irwin Hedges observed, neither the United States or Europe was in a position to negotiate down farm subsidies (pp. 65–66). Although the reasons for President Johnson's thinking remain unclear, Francis Bator suggests that he chose to "back away in the end from the U.S. commitment to a big bargain in agriculture . . . in order to make a big industrial bargain" (p. 68).

How do participants view the Kennedy Round thirty years later? STR Roth said he thought the round "turned out pretty well," but "I feel we were too lenient, and didn't bargain enough . . . with the Japanese" (p. 77). Robert McNeill, who served in the Commerce Department, suggested that "the settlement with Japan. . . . was one of the least reciprocal settlements among those with industrial countries" (p. 92). Michael Blumenthal defended the final arrangements in political terms: "We were in a way pioneers. This was a very different kind of negotiation. In political terms it was very important, because it occurred during the depths of the Cold War. The U.S.–European relationship, the strengthening of Europe, the frontier in the Cold War, was of great importance to the United States" (pp. 78–79).

White House deputy national security adviser Francis Bator sought to rebut criticism that the results proved asymmetrical. He rejected the notion that President Johnson gave away the store to get an agreement. The truth, he said, is complicated. "It is . . . entirely legitimate that the president of the United States should consider those trade-offs." He noted that concurrent negotiations were going on involving special drawing rights for increased international liquidity and on military issues such as force levels and offset arrangements. "So certainly those considerations played a role" (pp. 90–91). The Kennedy Round outcome, he said, contributed to "incremental problem solving" and strengthened the American hand during the Cold War, when the division of Germany and a rift between President de Gaulle and the United States posed threats (p. 107).

Did the United States obtain reciprocity in the Kennedy Round? Blumenthal observed that a numbers game occurs in every negotiation. "Since you can prove anything you want with numbers, I know that we proved decisively and definitely that we had total reciprocity at the end of the Kennedy Round with numbers. I suppose other people who would not wish us well could have proved the opposite. The numbers and measures used are sufficiently imprecise" (p. 82). Economist Ernest Preeg, who calculated the numbers on a borrowed IBM 360 computer, insisted, "These numbers were there." Noting the relationship between reciprocity and strategic thinking, he emphasized that the Kennedy Round was a "foreign policy initiative" (pp. 97–98).

One of the important lessons gleaned from experience in the Kennedy Round, Blumenthal suggested, was that the items that seemed to matter most at the time—chicken parts, Danish hams, and American selling price—had little long-term significance because basic economic forces continue to alter the marketplace (p. 95). Harald Malmgren agreed that "almost all of these politically sensitive issues turned out to be ephemeral" (p. 100). Yet, because they were prepared to carve out politically sensitive sectors, such as oil and textiles, which were excluded from concessions, U.S. officials were able to liberalize trade where they could.

Chapter 4 offers a retrospective on the Tokyo Round, the seventh round of multilateral negotiations, which concluded in 1979. This round involved ninety-nine countries and ended formally on April 12, 1979. Advanced countries agreed to cut tariffs about 33 percent on industrial goods. For the United States this meant reducing tariffs on dutiable manufactures from 8.1 percent to 5.6 percent. While some progress was made in opening the Japanese market to agriculture, the European Community blocked any effort to roll back the variable-levy system. The round also extended the GATT regime to cover nontariff barriers. Nations approved a series of specialized, nontariff codes pertaining to subsidies and countervailing duties, antidumping, technical barriers and product standards, government procurement, import licensing, customs valuation, and certain agricultural products. The broad purpose of these codes was to reduce the trade-distorting impact of domestic practices.

Once again the U.S.-European relationship drove the outcome. STR Bob Strauss vividly described his efforts at the beginning of the Carter presidency to organize the trade representative's office and to give the round new momentum. Negotiations were "dead in the water," he said (p. 117), but President Carter was determined that they succeed. Although the Department of Agriculture attached high priority to destroying the European common agricultural policy (CAP), Strauss concluded the United States must be more flexible if there was to be any agreement. He visited Brussels in July 1977 and indicated that the U.S. did not want to destroy or eliminate the CAP. This was the beginning, he said, of U.S.-European joint leadership for concluding the round.

Deputy STR Alan Wolff agreed: "We had a partnership with Europe and the fact is you need a partnership with the European Community to move major trade talks forward. It will not be moved with a partnership with Japan" (p. 136). Whereas conflicts between European Community and U.S. negotiators had sometimes disrupted the Kennedy Round, participants in this session maintained that a warm cooperative relationship developed between Sir Roy Denman, the European head of delegation, and Alonzo McDonald, his U.S. counterpart (pp. 131, 136).

Discussing the negotiations, McDonald, a business executive, explained that his own objective was to reduce government barriers, to reduce risk, and to create opportunities for individual investors. This point of view, a business perspective, flowered he says in the decade following the Tokyo Round. "During the ten years following the Tokyo Round the attitude of independent business decision makers as to what was an acceptable level of risk in international affairs . . . began to blossom. From my point of view that was the real accomplishment—and that was what we set out to achieve in Geneva with the Tokyo Round" (p. 134).

McDonald at times found it more exasperating to deal with Washington than with foreign negotiators. He described a triangle in which U.S. government agencies first had to negotiate a set of instructions to the U.S. delegation. Then the negotiations continued between Geneva and Washington. Finally, there were the actual negotiations with ninety-nine foreign governments. While dealing with Washington agencies was difficult, McDonald said, "Negotiating with the Japanese really involves the Chinese water treatment. It takes a great deal of persistence and patience, but there is almost nothing instantaneous. You have to go in tiny steps. We did. We dragged them along. We spent an awful amount of time with them" (p. 139).

What might the United States have done better? Former Commerce Department official Larry Fox said that in retrospect it was appropriate that the round should be labeled the Tokyo Round: The United States and Europe lacked a grand strategy for dealing with Japan and its network of nontariff barriers. The United States assumed Japan would mature into an open-market economy. John Greenwald argued that U.S. officials failed to understand the core problem stemming from Japan's government control over East Asian economic development. He said U.S. negotiators erred by focusing on Europe, and treating Japan as "the tail of the dog" (p. 143).

Asked to assess overall results, the participants disagreed sharply. USTR Strauss judged the Tokyo Round agreement to be a "good work product. I don't think any of us gave it A+. I think all of us gave it B+ or maybe an A–" (p. 120). But, John Greenwald, the most critical of the panel, graded the effort a D– or F+. He voiced concerns about whether the U.S. fought "the right war" and had "addressed the right issues." He also worried about the "conceit that international codes and conduct are going to end up being effective measures for disciplining international trade behavior" (p. 165). Former Treasury aide Gary Hufbauer disagreed, rating the results a B+. He contrasted favorably the self-enforcing international trading system with outmoded institutions of international finance. Alan Wolff praised the fast-track relationship with Congress, which he considered an "extraordinary accomplishment" after defeat of Kennedy Round agreements on American selling price and dumping, and defeat of the Russian trade agreement. The Tokyo Round, he added, gave GATT "legitimacy" in the sense that it was mentioned in the 1974 and 1979 trade acts (p. 167).

From the standpoint of labor, Howard Samuel said, the Tokyo Round fostered cynicism and suspicion among industrial workers because private interests struck special deals with the government concerning textiles and steel. "The hostility of much of labor to open trade, based on the belief that special interests usually trump the broad national interest, has not diminished since the Tokyo Round" (p. 169).

Once again the agriculture gains came up short of expectations. Dale Hathaway noted that although the Tokyo Round accomplished little for farmers, it did lay the groundwork for substantial changes in the Uruguay Round. State Department official Jules Katz viewed the Tokyo Round as one more element in a historic trade liberalization process begun in the 1930s. To businessman McDonald, the Tokyo Round was an "important step forward" and one that changed a lot of business attitude about international investments. The proportion of U.S. trade to GDP has doubled in the twenty years since the Tokyo Round. "I can assure you that the attitude of private business of taking risk to make investments across borders would be quite different if we had returned and said, We abort the whole thing, we cannot live in an international economy together, we have no hope" (p. 171).

From the three panel discussions, several significant and common themes emerged. They might be succinctly described as the importance of critical working relationships, vision, leadership, and persuasive individuals. During the GATT era perhaps the two most important relationships were between Congress and the executive, and the trans-Atlantic partnership with Europe. The constantly evolving, always delicate relationship between the executive and Congress shapes trade policy and every negotiation. Indeed, the two branches have struggled over trade policy intermittently since the Federalist period.

Friction between the two branches seems to have increased as Secretary of State Cordell Hull's reciprocal trade program succeeded in opening the U.S. market and lowering tariff levels. Hull and his aides in the State Department who managed the program preferred to think of themselves as "freer" traders, rather than free traders (p. 17). They also believed strongly in establishing an international trade organization to facilitate negotiations and to establish rules for international trade relations. But the Republican-majority Congress elected in 1946 did not share the executive branch's enthusiasm for membership in the ITO. Perhaps Senate Finance Committee Chairman Eugene Millikin and his supporters were "mindless," as Amy Porges suggested (p. 45), or perhaps they had a more traditional vision of national economic interests than did the executive.

Whatever the reasons for the conflict, the rift between Congress and the executive over trade policy widened during the 1950s. Congress again balked at membership in an international trade organization and diluted requests for trade-negotiating authority. As participants in the Kennedy Round session observed, the 1962 Trade Expansion Act compromised those differences. The executive obtained an unprecedented grant of negotiating authority, but Congress assigned responsibility for the negotiations to the newly created Special Trade Representative, who worked for the president but also reported to Congress. Late in the Kennedy Round tensions between the trade bureaucracy and Congress revived and led to congressional rejection of agreements negotiated on antidumping and American selling price valuation. Former State Department official Jules Katz suggests that the dispute with Congress demonstrated to the world that "we could not carry out the agreements we had reached" (p. 169).

A Democratic Congress chose not to renew the executive's tariff-cutting authority for seven years—until passage of the Trade Act of 1974. During this period the executive had no negotiating authority to enter multilateral negotiations on the emerging problems of nontariff barriers. The conflict between the legislative and the executive branches was not a traditional partisan one. The Johnson administration could not overcome the reservations of its political allies in Congress. Interestingly, in 1974 a Democratic Congress renewed trade negotiating authority while it was busy investigating and preparing to impeach a Republican president. But the terms of the bargain, which established a new fast-track negotiating procedure, made Congress an active participant in the negotiations. The 1974 act also directed the Special Trade Representative to establish a system of sectoral advisory committees to better gain input from affected constituencies. But the deal signaled trading partners that Congress would expedite its review of any international agreements the executive submitted.

As the discussion in chapter 4 suggests, the Carter administration did succeed in establishing a more productive relationship with Congress. In part, it reflected the people skills of STR Robert Strauss, who knew little about trade but had close personal ties to members of Congress, Democrats as well as Republicans. In his presentation Strauss recalled how Senators Russell Long and Abraham Ribicoff promised to make him a "hero" if he accepted the STR job. Deputy STR Wolff credits Strauss with making an enormous difference. Strauss "established lasting relationships with people he negotiated with. He knew he couldn't get more from them than they could deliver, and that defined the parameters of the negotiations. He taught us all quite a number of good lessons" (p. 168). While many of the participants considered the final Tokyo Round agreements "imperfect," experience with the new fast-track process helped lay the basis for continued cooperation during the Uruguay Round, when the executive negotiated broader agreements establishing the World Trade Organization and extending the rule of world trade law to agriculture and services.

Strauss and his aides also seem to have established a strong working relationship with European leaders in Brussels. Circumstances had changed since the Kennedy Round. Britain was now a member of the European Community, and General de Gaulle had retired from politics. Working together, after the United States abandoned plans to deconstruct the common agriculture policy, the new Atlantic partnership was critical to deal making in the Tokyo Round.

Another important theme raised by participants in the several sessions relates to the importance of American policy leadership. In looking back at the fifty-year history of GATT, several speakers emphasized the importance of the American vision for trade liberalization, and the willingness of the United States to support this concept with muscle. Amy Porges says she is "struck by the power of a single very corny word, *dreams.* This is a story in which believing it so has made it so. They got enough people together who really believed this would work, and it worked" (p. 45). To some extent, this vision was shared in other trading nations, particularly in the English-speaking world. The United Kingdom played an active role in the creation of the GATT system.

To effect a consistent program of trade liberalization over six decades, people with the right skills were indispensable. Margaret Potter-Leddy identified three distinct types: political leaders, idea persons, and negotiators and draftsmen. In the first category were Secretary of State Cordell Hull and Will Clayton, the Texas cotton exporter and State Department official who championed liberal trade during the Truman administration. The former zealously pressed for tariff liberalization; the latter pushed for GATT and international trade organization. Other politically connected leaders, such as George Ball and Robert Strauss, proved crucial to launching the Kennedy Round and completing the Tokyo Round. In the second category Potter-Leddy lists economists like Jacob Viner and Alvin Hansen. In launching the Kennedy Round, Mike Blumenthal notes, Raymond Vernon had great influence. Law professors, as well as economists, influenced the policy process. Legal scholars, such as John H. Jackson, a former general counsel of STR, pushed a complementary vision of a rule-oriented structure for the global marketplace. Jackson's ideas seem to have had considerable impact on the young lawyers who moved into policy and negotiating positions in the 1980s and negotiated the Uruguay Round.[3]

Among the influential negotiators and draftsmen Harry Hawkins stands in a unique category. As an adviser to Hull, he played a key role in launching the reciprocal trade program and preparing the way for an international trade organization. Subsequently, others like John Leddy and Carl Corse assumed these responsibilities. The GATT official who did most to shape the institution was Eric Wyndham White, the director general of GATT (1948–68), who presided over GATT's birth and establishment. His leadership was important in establishing GATT as a major player and in completing the Kennedy Round. Some of the U.S. panelists thought he moved too fast during the 1960s in admitting thirty or forty developing countries in response to pressure from the United Nations Conference on Trade and Development. In striving for universality, says Michael Smith, GATT admitted nations unable to accept their obligations or even to pay dues. As a result many new members became pawns in the GATT politics of former European colonial powers or accepted the direction of India and Brazil, which sought to lead less developed nations.

Discussion among panelists at the three ITC Historical Society sessions revealed some disappointments and frustrations. Some thought the United States should have done more in the Kennedy and Tokyo Rounds to open the Japanese market. Others thought the architects of the post-GATT system, based on the World Trade Organization, may have succumbed to the "conceit . . . that in nontariff barriers, codes of international conduct are sufficient disciplines . . ." (p. 165).

Despite some differences of emphasis, the former government officials seemed to agree that trade liberalization and the rule of law offered the best hope for achieving peace and prosperity. This perspective—the so-called Washington consensus in support of economic internationalism—continues to inspire U.S. officials as it has done for over sixty-five years—since Cordell Hull launched his program of trade liberalization. Indeed, in light of the protectionist policies that drove U.S. trade policy before the New Deal, the triumph of economic internationalism in America is one of the more important themes in twentieth-century history.

It is at least arguable that the trade policy professionals who conceived and negotiated the open global trading system after World War II should rank among the twentieth century's most successful revolutionaries. Political revolutionaries like Vladimir I. Lenin, Adolph Hitler, and Fidel Castro all attempted, and failed, to export revolutions and transform the established international order. But, the economists, lawyers, and trade negotiators who persistently pressed a laissez-faire vision of market forces binding nations together and promoting democracy had largely succeeded as the century neared its end. Their efforts, supported by U.S. economic and political leadership, brought the progressive dismantling of national trade barriers, the opening of markets, and the establishment of the World Trade Organization to structure the system and resolve disputes.

But were these accomplishments sustainable? As the twentieth century closed, some observers wondered if the deregulatory revolutionaries who fashioned the global trading system had overreached. Would the WTO's mandatory dispute resolution mechanism generally succeed in opening markets—particularly for agriculture and services? Would it arouse a backlash from those concerned about other values, such as national sovereignty, human rights, and environmental issues? Would public opinion celebrate the efficiency gains from growing integration of markets, or worry about economic insecurity, stemming from job dislocations, and inequality in income distribution? Could public dissatisfaction fuel protectionist counterrevolutions?[4] More generally, could the world trading system survive periodic bouts of destabilizing financial contagion? How the global trading and financial systems responded to such challenges in the years ahead will have significant bearing on how twenty-first-century scholars and policymakers evaluate the important trade policy undertakings analyzed in this volume.

✧ CHAPTER TWO

Is GATT Dead? A Retrospective

Participants: William T. Hart (Tariff Commission; ITC), William B. Kelly (GATT), Richard Matthiessen (USTR-Geneva), Douglas Newkirk (USTR), Amy Porges (USTR), Margaret Potter-Leddy (Department of State), and Michael Smith (USTR). This session took place October 27, 1997, at the U.S. International Trade Commission. The moderator was Alfred E. Eckes.

Alfred Eckes: This session attempts a retrospective assessment of the General Agreement on Tariffs and Trade (GATT). A half-century ago, in October 1947, the Geneva Round of tariff negotiations inaugurated the multilateral trade negotiating process under GATT auspices. Over the succeeding years there were seven other multilateral negotiations—concluding with the Kennedy Round (1964–67), the Tokyo Round (1973–79), and the Uruguay Round (1986–94).

In announcing this program, the ITC Historical Society suggested the theme: Is GATT dead? We thought it might attract more interest than the alternative: Is GATT alive? Although GATT no longer exists as an institution, I believe that many of our distinguished panelists will take the position that the spirit of GATT burns brightly in the new World Trade Organization.

To lay a foundation for our discussion, let me offer a few introductory comments. At the end of World War II the United States invited nineteen foreign countries, including the Soviet Union, to participate in a conference to negotiate a multilateral trade agreement which was to be the basis of a proposed International Trade Organization. Although the Soviets opted to pursue an autarkic course and did not participate, representatives of twenty-three countries did travel to Geneva and joined those negotiations. The tariff negotiations proceeded bilaterally among principal suppliers on a product-by-product basis. Concessions were extended generally on a most favored nation basis. Every country which chose to sign the agreement thus was eligible to enjoy the concessions of every other member and so gained unconditional most favored nation status.[1]

On January 1, 1948, nine countries, accounting at that time for 80 percent of world trade, put GATT into effect. These first members were: Australia, Belgium, Canada, Cuba, France, Luxembourg, the Netherlands, the United Kingdom, and the United States. As a temporary forum for trade negotiations, pending creation of the proposed International Trade Organization, GATT survived for nearly half a century.

Sometimes it seemed as if GATT was misnamed. Some commentators have suggested it should have been named GAB, since talk was the one commodity the international trade organization often seemed to have in abundance. GATT sometimes seemed long on discussion but short on action. Nonetheless, if one looks at the full record of the last fifty years, it is apparent that the GATT made an important contribution to the liberalization of trade barriers—especially in the reduction of tariff and nontariff barriers. During the eighth round of multilateral negotiations—the so-called Uruguay Round—participants agreed to establish a permanent World Trade Organization, and it succeeded GATT in January 1995. Today we will revisit the GATT record with a group of U.S. trade policymakers and negotiators familiar with all aspects of the GATT legacy.

An appropriate place to begin this discussion is with some consideration of GATT's origins. Why was GATT established and what difference did it make?

William Kelly: The short answer to why GATT was established is the United States. The U.S. emerged from World War II as the only strong commercial country. In that position it virtually dictated the rules for international trade in the postwar period. The

United Kingdom and a few other countries were involved in the preparations and implementation of what became the GATT, but it was really U.S. muscle that got GATT off the ground. That support continued throughout GATT's history. The U.S., especially some very dedicated people in the State Department, wanted an international trade organization to avoid the beggar-thy-neighbor commercial policies of the 1930s. The idea was to establish the International Trade Organization, which would lay down some trade rules and conduct negotiations to lower trade barriers. Meanwhile, the International Monetary Fund [IMF] would fix exchange rates and we would have a regime of fixed exchange rates that would avoid the competitive exchange rate depreciations of the 1930s.

As it turned out, the ITO charter, which was negotiated at the Havana Conference in 1948, never took effect. Instead, the General Agreement on Tariffs and Trade, an interim agreement, signed on October 30, 1947, by some twenty-three countries, endured. Not surprisingly, this agreement contained three fundamental principles of U.S. trade policy. The first was unconditional most favored nation [MFN] treatment. The second was elimination of quantitative restrictions for protective purposes. The third involved negotiations for lowering tariffs. Incidentally, this was not free trade and I wish the people in this [Clinton] administration—and out of it—would quit referring to the GATT and the WTO as organizations for free trade. There was nothing about free trade in the GATT or the WTO. It was freer trade. I might suggest that this identification would sit better with the U.S. Congress and the U.S. public.

I want to make several comments about the history of the three principles that underpin the GATT. In 1923, under the leadership of Secretary of State Charles Evans Hughes, the United States adopted the unconditional form of the most favored nation clause after adhering for 150 years to the conditional form. Article I of the GATT committed members to the unconditional most favored nation approach, and this principle became a foundation of the agreement. With regard to quantitative restrictions, the United States had participated in some League of Nations conferences during 1927 and 1928, which looked toward the elimination of quantitative restrictions for protective purposes. Not only did the United States participate in these conferences, but it signed the 1927 convention that abolished all import and export prohibitions and restrictions. There were a few exceptions, as there always are, but this was the convention that was negotiated and signed by the U.S. The Senate gave its consent to ratification, President Hoover ratified it, and proclaimed it into effect on the part of the United States in 1930. Because some countries did not ratify it, the agreement was only in effect a few years and the remaining participants, including the United States, soon withdrew. As I recall, they did so by 1934. The convention really galvanized the U.S. position in support of eliminating quantitative restrictions, and this is reflected in Article XI of the GATT.

In 1934 the Reciprocal Trade Agreements Act, associated with Secretary of State Cordell Hull, reversed the high nonnegotiable U.S. tariff and led to a series of bilateral trade agreements that reciprocally lowered U.S. and other countries' tariffs. These bilateral agreements all contained the unconditional form of the MFN clause. Between countries signing the agreement they abolished all quantitative restrictions on scheduled items (that is, on the items that were negotiated for tariff reduction). This principle of tariff reductions is now reflected in Article XXIX of the GATT.

To return to the theme of this session, I do not believe that GATT is dead. The GATT is really a multilateral extension of the bilateral U.S. trade agreements program. The World Trade Organization, which incorporates by reference the text of the GATT, is an extension of the GATT to other areas such as services. At long last [the WTO] provides an organizational home for the GATT which could not be realized in 1947. My final thought—or perhaps it should be a prayer—let us hope that the GATT continues in this home for another fifty years.

Margaret Potter-Leddy: I agree with what Bill Kelly said. Far from being dead the WTO is an extension of GATT, which was an extension of the bilateral reciprocal trade program, which was an extension of the most favored nation principle. To get all of this going, it really took three kinds of leaders. First, there had to be people who believed in freer trade and equitable conditions of trading and who had lots of political power. That was absolutely essential. Without Cordell Hull we would probably never have had the trade agreements program. Without Will Clayton, I don't know whether we would have gotten the GATT.

Kelly: Harry Hawkins, Clair Wilcox . . .

Potter-Leddy: I am coming to them. Harry Hawkins and Clair Wilcox are other examples of key people. On the first level, I had in mind leaders like Hull, Clayton, and Willard Thorp. At a second level, you had to have people with ideas, people who developed these generalities into real concepts. And in that class I would mention Jacob Viner, an economist who worked at the Tariff Commission in the 1920s, and Alvin Hansen, an economist who worked in the trade agreements division of the State Department in the 1930s. Hansen, incidentally, produced a notable student—Carl Corse. Carl was himself more of a teacher than a civil servant, but he acted as a civil servant.

On the third level were other individuals who converted these ideas into words and phrases that could be agreed upon internationally. They were the negotiators. On this level, the most important one was Harry Hawkins. Helping him with the drafting and the negotiations was not only Corse, but a young fellow who arrived from the Pan-American Union about the same time—John Leddy. He turned out to be a pretty good draftsman.

Eckes: Bill Kelly mentioned Charles Evans Hughes and the unconditional most favored nation policy. I think we should acknowledge the pivotal role of an official from the Tariff Commission in bringing about this change. William Smith Culbertson, the first vice chairman of the Tariff Commission, was very instrumental in bringing about the shift from the conditional to the unconditional most favored nation policy. He would later serve as ambassador to Chile during the Hoover administration.

Turning to the early years of GATT, it is my impression that GATT was largely run by the English-speaking nations, particularly the Americans and the British. Asian involvement did not come until much later. Japan entered GATT in 1955, but many of the other Asian countries did not join GATT until the 1980s. Why was GATT run by the Americans, the British, and the Canadians?

Kelly: GATT was a rich man's club. Some of us wish it had stayed that way! [laughter]

Amy Porges: One might add that a substantial part of the rest of the world had been bombed flat.

William Hart: Exactly. Until the 1950s mainland Europe was still recovering. Most of Asia, except for China, which was an original member of the GATT, was not active in the international trading system.

Eckes: But even after economic conditions improved, didn't the Japanese maintain a very low profile in GATT, one not proportionate to their real economic power?

Kelly: Very much so.

Porges: The Tokyo Olympics of 1964 marked the emergence of Japan onto the world stage. If you look at original Article XXVI it was written so that the GATT could not enter in force unless both the U.S. and the U.K. were on board. There was a requirement that members accounting for 85 percent of world trade had to sign up. Those percentages were geared so that the U.S. and the U.K. would have to be on board. Why? At that time the U.S. and the U.K. each accounted for 25 percent of world trade. At that time Britain and America were the two big actors in world trade. After all, this was the era before decolonization. At that time the U.K. stood for not only the United Kingdom but the United Kingdom and its colonies. It is no mystery that the GATT started out as a bipolar arena in which the U.S. and the U.K. were the two large actors. France was a discontented outsider.

Eckes: What do you recall about the attitudes of the developing countries? India and Brazil were involved in the 1947 negotiations creating GATT, but they remained vigorous critics of the GATT system through much of its history. Why?

Michael Smith: They still are [critical]. I don't agree with Kelly that the GATT was a rich man's club. I think GATT reflected the reality of the times. Certainly, in 1955 England was not a rich country. It had been devastated by the war. The United States was a rich country. France was not a rich country. They [Great Britain and France] were after all major recipients of U.S. aid during that period. It was a reflection of the times, as Amy

Porges said. GATT members were traders. This was a trading club, not a rich man's club.

With regard to India, it was brought in prematurely as one of the founding members. I say it was brought in prematurely because I do not think the British had inculcated in the Indian civil service a sense of what trade was all about. And this has nagged us ever since, as you know very well, Mr. Kelly. It certainly nagged me when I was in the government. The same thing applies to Brazil. Al [Eckes] asked about the developing countries. A lot of the decisions to admit developing countries were made on political grounds, which had nothing to do with their trading status. Until recently India and Brazil combined represented 3 percent of world trade, yet they were put on the same level as the United States and Japan. I think that [fact] has nagged the system.

Any of you who have gone through the Tokyo and Uruguay Rounds know what difficulties there were in getting Brazil to the bargaining table. We went through tremendous contortions to do that. One result is that when the Uruguay Round was finally enacted no exceptions were allowed. You either joined up for the whole thing or you were out. This is the way GATT should have functioned from the beginning.

Eckes: Let's turn to the Soviets and the Chinese. As noted earlier, the Soviets were invited to participate in postwar planning for an International Trade Organization, but they opted not to do so. By the end of GATT's tenure, in 1994, Taiwan, China, Russia, and a number of other governments in parts of the old Soviet Empire were knocking on the door. The irony of history is that some of the countries most hostile to GATT later applied for membership.

Would the history of GATT have been different had the Soviets joined in 1947?

Kelly: Yes, very definitely. GATT would have become very political. They would have demanded many positions in the secretariat. I would probably not have gotten [a position] there!

Smith: The Soviet refusal to join [in 1947] was an unknown blessing at that time, much as their decision to walk out of the United Nations Security Council was at the time of the Korean

War. I think Bill Kelly is absolutely right on this point. The GATT would have been become a political entity, much like the UN. Whatever effectiveness the GATT had would not have happened [if the Soviet Union had become a member]. I think we were very lucky that they were stupid enough to turn it down.

Porges: There was clearly a long period in the 1950s when people who were involved in the GATT thought it was threatened. If the Russians had been members, it would have been ten times worse.

Smith: I think there is one other element. By the 1950s the U.S. was certainly using trade as a tool in its arsenal against the threat, perceived or real, of the Communist world. Ironically, while we benefited from the Soviets not being in the GATT (it would have turned GATT into a UN Security Council, or General Assembly, by the 1960s), . . . [many believed] that the GATT was an arrow in the Western world's quiver, much like the Marshall Plan became.

Eckes: Perhaps we should consider the related question of U.S. commitment to an international trade organization. In 1947, as a result of planning begun during World War II, we proposed the International Trade Organization. But, when Congress did not authorize U.S. membership in the ITO after the Havana Conference, GATT became the principal institution for trade cooperation. During the 1950s the Eisenhower administration again tried to establish a formal international trade organization—this time named the Organization for Trade Cooperation [OTC]. It was another version of the ITO. Forty years later [1995] those efforts finally prevailed with establishment of the World Trade Organization. Would it have made a difference to the world trading system had we joined the ITO in 1948 or 1949, or joined the OTC in the mid-1950s?

Kelly: I don't think it would have made much difference really. True, we might have had an organization earlier, and this might have simplified some financial details. . . . But, fundamentally, I don't see how it would really have been very, very different. Of course, if you get into the political aspect, assuming the Soviet Union had been a member, then it becomes very political and is a different kind of situation.

Eckes: The proposed ITO had investment-related provisions; and it seemed to do more for dispute resolution than the GATT. Can one view the current WTO as a modern version of the old ITO?

Potter-Leddy: To some extent, yes. I think it is true that the GATT might have been a bit broader in scope if the ITO had been adopted. As far as the organizational part is concerned, the GATT had been drafted in a very clever way, so that there was a structure there even though it was not evident, and it was not evident to Congress, in particular! [laughter] In spite of everything, there was an organization early on. The little trick of capitalizing the Contracting Parties was a pretty cute trick, I thought, because it gave us an opportunity to have an organization without saying so. And, incidentally, I think it was Eric Wyndham White [director general of GATT] who thought up the idea of having a council in the 1960s. That also strengthened the organizational side of GATT.

Kelly: Let me respond to the question, Would the world have been different had the ITO come into existence? I don't think the world was ready [after World War II] for provisions relating to investments, and to services, and to some of the other things that the WTO is involved with today. Given the decimation of most economies after World War II, I don't think that you would have proceeded very far in areas other than the ones GATT did pursue. . . .

Would Japan have really acted any differently, for example, if there had been a WTO, or an ITO, or an OTC? I think Japan would have sat back on its haunches and played the same game it has played for many, many years. Would some of these other countries have really taken a different fundamental attitude because they were now part of an organization?

Eckes: Do you think that with a mandatory dispute resolution mechanism, such as in the present WTO, GATT might have succeeding in opening markets earlier?

Kelly: It might have broken down.

Smith: Never, never.

Porges: As a dispute person—I baby-sit the U.S. dispute settlements program in the WTO—I really agree that the world of the

ITO was not ready for a WTO-type dispute settlement mechanism. Look at the early years of the GATT and what you see is episode after episode of countries ducking and pushing and trying to nudge each other to try to eliminate measures, never trying to confront, always trying to avoid. Many obligations were entered into way ahead of the time that any country was seriously prepared to abide by them. The history of GATT is a history of aspirations, aspirations which at the time were vastly ahead of the readiness of governments to actually abide by those obligations.

But in the end I hope that the readiness to abide has caught up. What we are finding under the WTO is that there are many places in the world where similar aspirations exist, but governments haven't yet caught up. This is why there are so many disputes being brought by the United States.

Most of these disputes would never have been brought under the GATT. For one thing, the GATT dispute settlement really didn't have much machinery for dealing with disputes where the facts are unclear. GATT really had no infrastructure. I don't think the ITO would have had much infrastructure either for going out and investigating the facts. Dealing with the facts is the single biggest weak spot in the WTO dispute settlement.

We are beginning to catch up, but it really has taken fifty years.

Potter-Leddy: One thing about the GATT that we shouldn't forget is that it did prove to be a good place to work on nontariff barriers. This, in turn, led to the widening of obligations in the WTO. The GATT was flexible enough so that it provided the basis later for widening out.

Smith: I think one of the fundamental mistakes that the United States allowed in the GATT—I think it could have stopped it, but the U.S. chose not to—occurred in the rush of decolonization. We added thirty or forty members to the GATT at one fell swoop. We should never have done this, not only because these nations were not ready to [undertake such obligations], but because our European allies—particularly the French and the British—were able to use those colonies in a way that we could not, since we were not the primary power in those countries. As late as the 1980s, my former adversary, and still friend, Mr. Tran [Van Tinh], who was the EC's ambassador there, would go out and marshal all these forces with the implied [threat] if these forty or fifty countries didn't toe the European Community's normally protectionist line, that they would have cutoffs in their Lome [preferential] benefits, or items like that. I think we made a mistake in reaching for universality of the GATT in the period of the 1960s.

I think we made a mistake in trying to move from a trading entity. We never well defined it. We never really said it was a trading organization. Kelly calls it a rich man's club, but we made a mistake in trying to make it into something it really wasn't. A good half of the members never showed up at GATT council meetings. A good half of the members didn't even know where GATT was. I think they had to pay minimal dues of $26,000 in those days. In one case involving an African country, the dues were sent from the country's capital to Geneva, and they kept in business a large number of houses of ill repute in Geneva. So much for GATT dues.

Kelly: Mike, I think you agree with me that maybe the GATT should have remained a rich man's club, and if you don't like that title I'll take whatever title you want to give it.

Smith: I don't like the title but I think we would have moved the ball farther, faster. Sure, we would have got some slings in the *New York Times* that we were excluding people. But there were lots of countries that just weren't ready. Indeed, we had sort of the reverse reaction. Some of the countries lined up politically in a third world group. It wasn't until the Uruguay Round that they came around. You remember the working paper that established the Uruguay Round was the first time that a number of the developing countries parted ways from the hegemony of the Indians and the Brazilians. And they went off on their own and said, "No, we are not going to buy this. Trade is in our interest. We are not going to follow the party line any more." I think we lost ten or fifteen years because of this thinking.

Douglas Newkirk: But in that context, Mike, you should point out that starting with Mexico's accession in 1986, we entered into serious negotiations on not only their tariffs, but nontariff measures, licensing systems, everything. And all of the subsequent accession negotiations—including all the Central American countries that have joined—have all had the same strict rules. What is going on now with Russia, China, and the other twenty-seven countries that are in line to join the WTO is the same kind of negotiation we initiated with the Mexicans.

Smith: But that gets back to Margaret's [Potter-Leddy] point that it took a political decision. Mexico, don't forget, first turned down GATT membership, and we went through hell. We had offered them everything but the kitchen sink, I think, and [Steve] Landy offered them that. And they turned it down. It was only when the Mexican government sucked in its gut and said this is the right way to go that it worked. I think the Mexican Revolution, if you will, is as profound—at least in international economic terms—as the Russian Revolution was in terms of coming to grips with international reality.

Porges: Let me raise a related point about what would have happened if the ITO had been implemented. If you look at the organizations, there was a period shortly after World War II that was highly optimistic and creative. People created international organizations to solve problems. The basic problem in creating an organization is how do you reconcile the sovereign equality of nations with the fact that some nations are in fact contributing more, and really need to have more of a say, or else you really are not going to get them on board. You are not going to have them as active members during the life of the organization sustaining it in the way that you want.

How do you reconcile the two concerns? There are a number of possible solutions. The Bretton Woods organizations—the [World] Bank and the [International Monetary] Fund—used weighted voting. Most functional UN organizations—such as the World Health Organization and the Food and Agriculture Organization—have an executive board which has certain permanent members and then some members selected on a geographical formula. I think the ITO also had this formula of having an executive board.

During the negotiation of the ITO there must have been an extensive discussion of whether it was possible to have weighted voting. Eventually weighted voting was rejected. In fact, the intersessional committee in the GATT—all the way through the 1950s—was really a body of limited membership. You had to be elected to the intersessional committee. The council was the first organ in the GATT that was basically a plenary organ. An organ that anyone could belong to, although not all parties did. Any country could become a member of the council, which was prepared to take on the responsibilities of membership—that is, the responsibility of showing up for meetings. The delegations that didn't have a mission in Geneva generally weren't members of the council. Basically, the council included everybody. The fact that the council included everybody meant that it became impossible in 1971, when Olivier Long [director general of GATT] tried to establish a limited body like an executive board, to move things forward. This might have been an effective counterpart to the [structure of the] IMF and World Bank.

During the period after the dollar floated, when the IMF was debating its future, I believe there was a debate in the GATT on how to dialogue with the fund. Long tried to set up an organ of limited membership; he failed. There have been various attempts over the years—most recently in the Uruguay Round by the United States—to set up limited membership committees on which the U.S. would have a seat, and certain other parties would have a permanent seat, and other seats would be allocated by geographical representation. The closest to this was the old CP-18, which was a very useful group. Perhaps Mike Smith has good memories.

Smith: I can't believe that you could say that the CP-18 was useful. [laughter]

Porges: All right, but it existed. The question is, Was it better than having nothing at all?

Eckes: What did CP-18 stand for?

Porges: The Consultative Group of Eighteen Contracting Parties.

Smith: There weren't eighteen, though. There were eighteen countries, plus the European Community, which at that time had nine members. Each one had to have two representatives. So Kelly-san helped preside over a group now called the Olivier Long memorial group, in which there were seventy or eighty people. It was a disaster. My greatest act in USTR was to get us out of that thing.

Porges: Basically the CP-18 died at the start of the Uruguay Round. That points to the fact that things move forward in small groups, and this has been the major problem organizationally for the GATT, and to some extent the WTO. Every one of the organs of the WTO is a plenary organ, a committee that everybody can belong to. Except for one, which is the Budget Committee. In fact, a lot of the important decisions are made in the Budget Committee.

Kelly: To get anything done—which means agreed upon—you have to have credible players. The problem is that we had a lot of uncredible players, some of them were incredible in fact. I am talking now about the developing countries. There were a bunch of [diplomatic] hangers-on who really had no instructions from their capitals. They really didn't want anything to happen, but they did want to be involved, always involved. That's the problem with the CP-18.

The problem is trying to get credible players around so that something happens. If you have those who don't want anything to happen, who are unwilling to make any commitments, have no authority to make any commitments, they gum up the works. That gummed up GATT for many years. Now, as was indicated, the Brazilians and Indians have changed. It is unbelievable to me to see this turnaround, but apparently they have finally figured out that they have a big interest in trade, and they are now credible players. In my day, they were not.

Porges: To recapitulate, the diffusion of the players, the diffusion of the membership, and the lack of any kind of executive board adds up to either paralysis or to real emphasis on gaining consensus, the kind of talismanic importance that was attached to consensus in 1994 when the Uruguay Round Agreements Act was pushed through.

Potter-Leddy: I want to say one thing about how unfortunate it was that the GATT got too many developing countries in it too early. I think we should remember that UNCTAD [United Nations Conference on Trade and Development] had a very bad effect on [Eric] Wyndham White. It made them [the GATT leadership] think that they must get into the development business too. This is how all these additional articles got added to the GATT, and it was a very bad business, I think.

Smith: I couldn't agree with you more.

Potter-Leddy: Purely bureaucratic business too—I mean just jealousy of a new agency coming in.

Smith: I keep thinking that maybe one morning I will wake up and read in the newspaper, or maybe now go on-line, and find out that TAD, as I used to call UNCTAD, has been abolished. But when I was over there, the GATT had 320 or 330 people, and UNCTAD had 1,800 people. It was mind-boggling. It had a building which was one of the biggest buildings in Geneva, and to my knowledge to this day they have done nothing.

Kelly: UNCTAD took some heat off of the GATT. Because the ambassador could go over to the UNCTAD and make a long speech, send a cable back to Buenos Aires, or wherever, saying, "Boy, I really told those developed guys to go to hell today." And then the ambassador could come over to the GATT and relax, because his capital had seen that he was doing the kind of job he was supposed to do in Geneva.

Eckes: Did the addition of all of the developing countries in the 1960s and 1970s accentuate the free-rider problem [by which developing countries enjoyed the concessions of others but offered few in their own markets]?

Smith: Sure, it did in principle. In fact, most of these countries didn't trade.

Eckes: But some have subsequently become important players in world trade.

Smith: In the 1960s it didn't hurt us. By the 1980s it was not a healthy thing. There were too many free riders in the sense that countries which could have assumed some obligations were not doing so. They were ducking out under the various provisions of Part IV, which apply to developing countries. That was unfortunate. I remember when I was at USTR and [Fred] Bergsten at that time was over at Treasury and [Richard] Cooper was over at State. They were going to go along with the new international economic order, which of course would have devastated the GATT. It would have finished GATT because it would have put the entire international economic system under an UNCTAD-type system, at a time when the old Brazilians and the old Indians were reigning supreme in Geneva and at UNCTAD.

Fortunately, I think USTR was able to block any effective participation in the new international economic order. But that was probably the apex of the free-rider concessions. In the last couple years of the Carter administration, and certainly in the Reagan administration and subsequently, officials have been very sensitive to the free-rider issue. Why? Because increasingly now a number of those developing countries have become traders. One must remember that the GATT, now the WTO, is not simply a bunch of concessions. It also involves a number of obligations. Members often forgot the obligations part and remembered only the concessions part. Back in the 1960s I don't think it hurt us. I think when [Doug Newkirk] was trying to do tariff negotiations, the free-rider problem, became more severe for him to handle—and for all of us.

Kelly: It is interesting that at the beginning of the GATT all of the countries that were signatories were in effect free riders, except for the U.S. and Canada.

Smith: Right.

Kelly: The U.S. made 50-percent tariff cuts that were effective. Others made tariff cuts in a reciprocal trade negotiation, but for balance of payments reasons those concessions were never applied. I agree with Mike [Smith] that there was a lag later on as far as the free-rider problem is concerned. But if you negotiate on the basis of the principal supplier rule, as we did under the pre–World War II reciprocal trade program, and which continued into the multilateral phase of tariff negotiations after the war, you didn't give an important concession to a country that had a very minor interest. Yes, some countries got the benefit through the unconditional MFN clause of these [tariff cuts], but I don't see it as a very big problem. I can't comment on Mexico but I think Doug and some other people, including the GATT, have done a great job on Mexico.

Newkirk: I want to add two points. One of the reasons that developing countries—big ones like India and Brazil—felt they could sit on the sidelines and cause trouble was not because of tariff questions but because of the obligation questions, a matter that Mike Smith raised. They didn't feel that they had any interest or any stake in the obligations. It didn't mean anything for them, so they felt that they had nothing to lose by making it difficult for developed countries to improve obligations in the Tokyo Round. By the middle of the Uruguay Round, they suddenly realized that they were becoming big trading partners, and had some interest in these obligations and codes—particularly the codes. They started behaving in a responsible manner. I think what really brought the change in attitudes was their own self-interest and their realization of what those interests were.

On the Mexican question, we were lucky to hit the Mexican accession negotiations at a time when they were negotiating with the IMF and the [World] Bank to obtain a little money. [laughter] The fund and the bank were asking them to do the same things that we were asking the Mexicans to do. Mexico accepted our position with only minor changes, because it killed two birds with one stone. It got them into GATT in time for the Punta del Este meeting, which was one of their political objectives, and also it took care of their problems with all three international institutions at the same time.

What followed from that example was a pattern. When we started an accession negotiation, we would go to the acceding country and say, This is what Mexico did. We expect the same thing from you. And one of those things, incidentally, was binding all of their tariffs at the time of accession. That was something quite new. Most of the countries that have come in subsequently have totally bound tariffs. Before Chile and Mexico acceded, that didn't happen. So the recent accessions have been quite different from the previous accessions.

Eckes: Let me raise another topic. We have heard about two directors general of GATT, Olivier Long and Eric Wyndham White. Perhaps it is also appropriate to talk about some of the individuals that contributed most to the development of GATT. Who were the most important ones?

Potter-Leddy: One would be Eric Wyndham White. He was a very talented guy and loved complicated, byzantine arrangements. But that was partly because he couldn't do anything if he didn't do it in a round-about way. He would go to the representative of India or Canada—they were his favorite tools—and get them to put ideas forward and to get support for those ideas. Sometimes that would lead to acceptance of his idea or sometimes it would bring up alternatives which he had in mind all along, but hadn't brought up. He was a terribly clever guy, devoted to the GATT.

Hart: I think that Wyndham White was absolutely necessary to the initial success of the GATT.

Eckes: He was British by background? Wasn't there a tradition of having British leaders in GATT?

Kelly: No, the tradition was never to have someone from the United States or the European Community.

Eckes: But always an American in the number two position, correct?

Smith: The tradition was that you always had a European as the number one person and at least one deputy from the United States. It is not written in concrete. Bill Kelly and I can remember when a former U.S. trade representative exploded when he found out whom people had agreed to make the director general as an outcome of one of the rounds. I think what has unfortunately happened—hopefully it has been taken care of now—is that the Europeans have come to think that the director general of GATT is their God-given right. That has had some unfortunate repercussions. Hopefully that thinking is over.

Kelly: Going back to the question about individuals who shaped the GATT, certainly Wyndham White would be on any short list. I think Margaret and I might share the same view. I didn't like his politics or his political pressure when he thought he had to expand the GATT membership to developing countries, because of UNCTAD. That is the only thing I would fault. The man was extremely talented in negotiations, in prodding everyone at the table. He would embarrass the ambassadors who weren't doing anything. He would find out whether you were or were not. He had his sources. Among other key people, I think that you must include U.S. leaders for pushing the GATT initially. You might include some of the people that Margaret mentioned earlier, as well as James Meade, who was involved on the British side.

Eckes: He is the Nobel laureate in international economics from Cambridge University.

Potter-Leddy: Harry Hawkins.

Kelly: Harry Hawkins, absolutely. I put John Leddy on the list too. John was at the Havana conference and he did a lot of the drafting on the GATT agreement itself.

Eckes: Anyone from developing countries that stands out?

Smith: I don't think you can say there was any person of great stature from the developing world, certainly until recently. They didn't play. Julio LaCarte-Muro [Uruguay] liked it, enjoyed life in Geneva, and was very articulate. But, quite frankly, I don't think any of the developing country leaders or their subordinates made any great mark. [They weren't] of the same stature as Wyndham White. Also, I think that had Arthur Dunkel [director general of GATT] not summoned up the political courage to issue what became the Dunkel Report, you would not have an Uruguay Round agreement today. I don't know who pushed him to issue that paper at a time when the Uruguay Round was going nowhere. I think that showed a flash of brilliance and leadership and I think due note should be made of that.

Porges: From the dispute settlement side, I would mention that LaCarte-Muro is the fellow who cooked up the Uruguay recourse where the Uruguayans sued many developed countries in the early 1960s for restricting temperate zone agricultural exports, basically. And this was a real turning point in the history of dispute settlement in the GATT. From examining the documents it really looks like a milestone.

Eckes: Let's focus on the broad accomplishments of GATT, measured in terms of the eight multilateral rounds. Obviously, they began at Geneva, followed by Annecy and Torquay, and several more rounds at Geneva, including the Dillon Round that ended in 1962, the Kennedy Round, Tokyo Round, and Uruguay Round. Which of the negotiating rounds were most significant and why? The textbook accounts seem to give emphasis to the first Geneva Round and the Kennedy Round in terms of the depth and breadth of tariff cuts. The Tokyo Round and the Uruguay Round moved in new directions. How do you, as GATT professionals, evaluate those eight rounds of multilateral negotiations?

Kelly: Four rounds stand out. One was the original GATT negotiation in 1947, which got things going on tariffs and set up the trade rules. The second was the Kennedy Round, where they ended the selective item-by-item approach to across-the-board tariff cuts, and employed an entirely different approach to tariff negotiations. Third, the Tokyo Round, where participants negotiated on nontariff barriers in a serious way which had not been possible in the previous Kennedy Round because of U.S. domestic legislation. And last, the Uruguay Round, which has gotten into all these new areas.

But suppose none of these rounds had happened. I wonder what the U.S. economy would look like today. I think we would have such a misallocation of resources that we could not possibly have the kind of growth and the dynamic economy that we have today. So the real benefits of the GATT process are the efficiencies in U.S. and foreign production that have led to higher standards of living and growth. It is interesting that world trade has grown even faster than GNP in these countries.

Smith: I don't think anyone of us around this table would differ. Those four rounds were pivotal to past successes and to the future hopes of the WTO. I think the jury is obviously still out on the Uruguay Round in the sense of whether we bit off too much to chew. I don't think so, but the jury is still out on that one.

There is a certain inevitability about the rounds, like the peeling of an onion. Tariffs were the first layer of the onion, and then quantitative restraints. It was obvious by the time the Tokyo Round came around, certainly for the developed world, that tariffs were less important and other barriers assumed higher importance. The evolution of the negotiations was inevitable. The great question for me, which is not on our agenda for today, except in the broadest sense, is the question that the traders have to think about in the months ahead: What is next? Is there a next? I don't believe that the GATT or the WTO is dead. It is just a question of what they do for encores.

Newkirk: I think you could argue that the Kennedy Round, Tokyo Round, and Uruguay Round slid into one another. It was a continuum. Once the tariff formula concept got started, it was picked up and carried forward. The concept of dealing with nontariff measures, which started in the Kennedy Round, particularly the work program between the rounds, focused on those nontariff measures. The primary codes were finally negotiated in the Tokyo Round, then refined in the Uruguay Round, and then became part of the WTO. These negotiations flowed together, particularly if you look at the work programs between the rounds.

If you look at what is going on now in the WTO, that work is continuing. One point that I would make in regard to Mike Smith's comment about the future is this: If you look at what has happened recently in the WTO, there have already been two new agreements approved without a round. That approach may suggest the future.

Smith: Right, absolutely. I couldn't agree more.

Newkirk: One other final point. If you conclude that GATT is not dead but rather is the soul of the new WTO, I think that you would have to mention the accomplishments of Peter Sutherland [director general of GATT] to wind up the Uruguay Round and start the WTO.

Eckes: You seem to think that the recent Financial Services Agreement will go forward despite the Asian currency meltdown. Is this financial turbulence only a temporary barrier, or is it going to lead to Asian currency blocs, new yen blocs?

Smith: I don't think we are there yet. Until USTR and the Treasury Department have their truce, or their coming together, nothing meaningful is really going to happen in financial services. Someone was talking about trying to bring people together of an earlier age. Doug [Newkirk] will remember when Bill Brock hosted a dinner for the trade and finance ministers of sixteen countries. It was held at a fancy restaurant in Paris, and some of the trade ministers had, I think, never met their finance ministers. And they have never met them since. That was a onetime show, and I think Don Regan was secretary of the treasury at that time. The hostility between USTR and Treasury on that issue was very clear, and I think before we see truly meaningful international agreements—which stop meltdowns, if you will—there is going to have to be an internal agreement among some of these countries where the trade people are not asked to enter via the rear door into the finance ministry. This happens in a number of countries, including this country.

Potter-Leddy: Apropos of that, I would like to ask, How are relations between the WTO and the IMF? I never thought that the GATT and the IMF cooperated enough.

Porges: There was a curious episode at the end of the Uruguay Round. Under Article XV of the GATT the IMF basically has the last word about claims that imports quotas were justified for balance of payments purposes. At the end of the Uruguay Round the IMF caught on to the fact that there were a number of agreements, like the TRIPS [trade-related aspects of intellectual property rights] agreement, that had no clause giving the IMF the last word. In fact, during the negotiation of the General Agreement on Trade in Services, they had shown up and had extracted such a clause, a clause that basically gave the IMF among other things carte blanche to authorize restrictions on payments for services whenever it suited them, as it does from time to time. The IMF caught on to the fact that there were some agreements that did not have such a trapdoor in them. The IMF raised a terrible fuss. Indeed, this occurred after the close of negotiations. This was during February and March of 1994, and the assembled delegations basically refused to reopen the agreement.

The result was an essentially meaningless declaration which is attached to the WTO agreement. It says the relationship between the IMF and the WTO will be the same as the relationship between the IMF and the GATT. It doesn't say anything about what the legal obligations are and whether the IMF actually has the same kind of legal relationship. It is basically a meaningless declaration.

So how are relations between the IMF and the WTO? There is in fact a formal bilateral agreement. There is information sharing; the GATT shares its data base on nontariff trade barriers with the bank and the fund. The GATT can draw on the economic expertise of the fund. The IMF cooperates in balance of payments consultations. And the fund has been fairly constructive to draw a line under fifty years of GATT history. The fifty years of GATT history has involved fifty years of balance of payments quotas for India.

In January of this year the IMF representative was asked the right questions at a balance of payments committee meeting.

The fund representative delivered the opinion that balance of payments quotas by India are completely unjustified and that in fact India would be much better off economically without them. And there, like a soap bubble breaking, went the legal justification for those balance of payments quotas under Article XV.

Yes, there is cooperation of a sort, and it is moving forward. I don't know if relations are particularly warm, but they never have been. I believe that the WTO, as part of the bilateral agreement between the WTO and the IMF, now has for the first time the ability to sit in on certain meetings of the executive board of the fund. I don't know how important it is substantively, but it is of great symbolic importance.

Kelly: Let me make a comment. I never found any big problems between the GATT and the fund. I think the last thing the trade people in the GATT wanted to do was to get into bed with the fund. Just like the trade people in the U.S. government would never want to get into bed with the Treasury, because the Treasury people are essentially not interested in trade and what you are trying to accomplish in this area. What they want to do is to use trade as a tool for balance of payments reasons, for exchange rate fluctuations, etc. I always wondered, despite all the language that appears in IMF and other reports about the need for closer cooperation between the GATT and the fund, I don't know what in the hell that was supposed to be. The fund would come over and we would have those balance of payments consultations. You would take the fund guy out to lunch. The consultations last a day and nothing happens. And then they go back to Washington. I thought this was rather ideal.

Eckes: Let's have some questions from the audience.

Question from audience: How did the GATT, a temporary organization pending establishment of the International Trade Organization, become a permanent organization without the approval of Congress?

Smith: I think the answer to this question is that the U.S. willed it. It was a nifty little device to come up with the phrase "Contracting Parties." This was a way to get around taking GATT to the Senate of the United States. Successive U.S. administrations persuaded everybody that GATT was a contract. When I was in the State Department, or when I was in USTR, we used to argue with the business community, or the people who opposed us. Why are we doing this? What legal obligations do we have? Well, it's a contract you know. The United States doesn't break contracts. Little did they know the real facts. To return to what Bill Kelly said, it was the United States that willed it so. They found some sympathetic people in the European Community, such as Finn Gundelach, who had a similar commitment.

At one point we used to have a trivia question, Which was the only country to ever ratify the GATT? That was Haiti. [laughter] I am sure now that other countries have ratified the GATT, but we didn't. We got around the awkwardness [with the notion of a contract]. I still think it goes back to what Margaret said at the very beginning: it was political leadership. The U.S. had the political will to make GATT work. And we bluffed it long enough so that it came into being through the back door. We put one piece after another into legislation and over successive enabling acts, or whatever the pieces of legislation that put the concessions into effect are called, the term GATT finally got into the legislation. So, if you will, it happened by osmosis. I remember Bill Kelly proposed at one time that we go up to the Hill and persuade Congress to ratify the GATT. Do you remember that, Bill?

Kelly: No.

Smith: You did. [laughter] We said, No way. This was when he was deputy director general of GATT. And he could say that. We shied away from that, preferring to let the sleeping dogs lie. One U.S. administration after another hid behind the concept of Contracting Parties, saying we had a legal obligation, we had a legal obligation, we had a legal obligation, we had a legal obligation. In fact, it was questionable whether we really did have an obligation.

Eckes: When you say the U.S. willed it, Mike Smith, you are in effect saying the executive branch did. Are you suggesting there was too much opposition on Capitol Hill, such as Senator Eugene Millikin [chairman of the Senate Finance Committee]?

Smith: No. There were people like Wilbur Mills [chairman of the House Ways and Means Committee], who helped will it. Later, Bill Frenzel [R-Minn.] and Sam Gibbons [D-Fla.] helped will it. It was more of a will than a conscious single document saying the United States ratifies the GATT.

Kelly: I question this lack of political judgment on my part. [laughter] In line with what you were saying, when I first joined the State Department, way back in 1951, I found myself immersed in a group of very dedicated people. These people were religious zealots as far as the GATT was concerned. Some of them are here today. Margaret is one of them. Bernie Norwood, in the audience, is another one. Others included Carl Corse, Leonard Weiss, Joe Greenwald, and Walter Hollis.

Potter-Leddy: Let's not forget Walter.

Kelly: All of these people had GATT as their main mission in life. They were a dedicated and talented group. In fact, they were so dedicated and talented that the Congress finally decided they better take the responsibility for dealing with GATT away from them and give it to the STR. [laughter]

Porges: Yes, that's the point, it certainly wasn't [President] Eisenhower or anybody in the Eisenhower White House. It wasn't [President] Truman in the end. I mean this is a great story of the ball being dropped time and time again at the highest level of the U.S. government. The U.S. government failed to push through the ITO when the time was right, and then they said the Marshall Plan had to go first. Then, the time was wrong, and the ITO failed. And then they failed to push through the OTC. The only explanation that I ever heard as to why the OTC did not go through in 1956 was that the Eisenhower administration decided that its real priority that year was a foreign aid bill, and they weren't going to push. . . . They actually had a bill to approve U.S. participation in the OTC all ready to go, all ready to report out of Ways and Means. Wilbur Mills was ready to shove it through the House of Representatives, and it wasn't an administration priority. Indeed, it is the people at this table that we have to thank for the fact that there were a cadre of people who grew up saying it is a contract, it is binding.

Kelly: To clarify a point, GATT was technically the interim commission for the International Trade Organization. That was its legal purpose. When Arthur Dunkel became director general they had to have a meeting of the interim commission on the

ITO. People had to figure out who was on this interim commission. China happened to be on the interim commission. Of course, China had withdrawn from the GATT but China was still around. This was a problem. But the interim commission had to meet. Because that was the legal basis for the GATT. It was never an organization, as Bernie says, because we couldn't join an organization with the trade agreements authority.

Porges: The interim commission still exists. I think the last time it met was for the coronation of [Renato] Ruggiero [director general, WTO]. In fact, it is a unique body. France belongs, but the European Community does not have a seat. It drives the European Commission crazy.

Smith: I come back to the point that leadership is critical in something like trade. Whether it was the cadre at the State Department or their successors elsewhere in the government, I don't quite buy the notion that Eisenhower and Truman weren't responsible. Because ultimately it all comes to the White House. We all know it does; and fortunately one president after another at least has not blocked it.

The presidents let the bureaucrats do their thing, which was the right thing. Today it is much different. You have an act of Congress; you have all this stuff enshrined in law, but, as you say, one guy could have killed it. It didn't happen. It didn't happen because there was enough of a political will in those very dangerous and vulnerable times that we just made it happen. They were great days, I think.

Kelly: Having gone through the logrolling of the Hawley-Smoot Tariff Act, the Congress passed the Reciprocal Trade Agreements Act in 1934 because they didn't want this trade issue anymore. They wanted the president to deal with trade. Then they could snipe at the corners, but they no longer had responsibility for his actions.

Smith: There still is no power in the world, apart from the United States, that has the clout to make something like the WTO work. It is up to us. You can point your finger wherever you want. But the gut question for international traders these days is, Is the United States going to exercise leadership in international trade? I would submit the jury is very, very much still out.

Eckes: Haven't we agreed to a voting formula in the WTO that in effect gives everyone one vote, except the European Community, which has the effect of returning to an United Nations General Assembly-type approach.

Smith: I would submit that they can have all the voting process in the world. If the United States wants to dig in its heels in the WTO, and stood alone, and was willing to make its membership a key issue, the WTO would bend, and rightly so. We make it work. It's not that we pay the most dues; as a matter of fact, we sometimes don't pay our dues, but it is our intellectual drive that keeps it going.

Eckes: What about the significance of Chinese membership?

Smith: The Chinese issue dates back to at least the 1950s. If China were to come in and make an honest, realistic application, the Europeans, Japanese, and Americans could put aside the geopolitics of it all.

Does China change the situation? Perhaps. There is a danger here. It looks awful funny to look at the world map. Remember the old days when the British Empire was all pink? Well, now you have the GATT empire, or the WTO empire, which is all pink, except this very large blank area in Russia and this very large blank area in China. There are some who argue that China shouldn't come in. They would say that the basic presumption of a free-market economy, or of working toward free-market principles, is not there. But that's water over the dam.

The negotiations are going on. Whether or not they actually do satisfy sufficient terms is again, I would hasten to add, our decision. If China doesn't satisfy the United States, its membership won't see the light of the day.

Eckes: As we bring this session to a conclusion, let me invite each of our panelists to offer a concluding thought about the significance of GATT.

Newkirk: First, let me add something to what Mike Smith said about China. I spent six frustrating years trying to negotiate their accession, and at the end of that time they were no farther ahead than the day we started. There seems to be evolving two schools of thought. One is make them comply with the GATT and then let them in. The other school of thought says let them in and then try to make them comply. If that second school of thought prevails, which is a political school of thought, I think it would have very serious detrimental implications for the WTO.

Moving from that, when you discuss whether or not the GATT has made a significant impact on the world trading system, one can't start with the GATT and work forward. One must start with the world trading system and the world commercial system, and look down to see what role GATT had in developing this system. In all probability the world trade regime and the [rising] volume of world trade would have taken place with or without the GATT. It really is a question of whether the GATT assisted in this phenomenal growth in world trade since World War II. I think the answer is yes. The GATT provided a framework, a sense of security, and transparency for a large portion of world trade, particularly among developed countries. I think now with the WTO that [approach] is going to spread more and more among the entire world—all 130 current members and 27 applicants. There will be security and certainty in the conduct of international trade.

Potter-Leddy: What Doug said reminds me of a remark my father made to me a long, long time ago. It was when we were still negotiating bilateral trade agreements. He said, "What in the world is the sense of negotiating all these agreements. Why didn't President Franklin Roosevelt just reduce the tariff? Anybody who could have closed the banks could have reduced the tariff." [laughter]

Kelly: He never would have gotten away with it.

Potter-Leddy: I don't think he would have either.

Kelly: It wouldn't have been a good idea, because we would then have no chips to play in getting other countries to do something.

Potter-Leddy: But the point was, there was no other way to get dollars but by trading with us.

Kelly: With 25 percent unemployment in the United States at the time, I don't think [it was possible].

Potter-Leddy: My father may have had a point, but I don't think Roosevelt could have gotten away with it either.

Kelly: He didn't pack the Supreme Court successfully; he tried that too, you know. Anyway the accomplishments of GATT, when you look at them from a statistical point of view: You have the

Hawley-Smoot average tariff rates of the United States of 50 percent; we are down to less than 5 percent now. I just wonder what the world would look like without the GATT and without this entire U.S. trade agreements program that has gone on for more than sixty years now. We no longer have American selling price for customs evaluation. It has been negotiated away and we have gotten reciprocal concessions.

We don't know what would have happened without the GATT. I'm not so sure, Doug, that the GATT facilitated what would have happened anyway. Given the beggar-thy-neighbor policies of the 1930s—both in the exchange rate and in the trade field—there was no guarantee in the postwar period that the United States was going to turn away from its protectionist policies, from its isolationist policies, and lead the world in this new global trading system. This was not a given. The GATT is what brought that about, and it benefits everybody—particularly for the United States. I am always for more benefits for us than for anyone else.

Smith: I would make four points. First, regarding the significance of the GATT, there was a certain inevitability to the expansion of trade. But there was not an inevitability to the liberalization of the terms of trade. That is what the GATT did. Anybody could reduce tariffs which are fairly cut and dried, and talk about the expansion of trade. I used to have terrible arguments with Sir Roy Denman, who always insisted that the purpose of the GATT was the expansion of trade. I would also come back and say, "No, no, the purpose of the GATT is the liberalization of the terms of trade." I would say that is the greatest thing.

Second, the GATT kept the protectionist instincts of both the Americans and the Europeans in check. This country has had a two-hundred-year tradition of protectionism. GATT keeps us from acting in accordance with our worst instincts. But our dear European allies have as much, if not more, tendencies toward protectionism. The Common Market is the first break in a thousand years.

Finally, I would have hoped that President Bill Clinton made reference to the fact that this week or next is the fiftieth anniversary of it all. It would have been nifty to have the president of the

United States go to Geneva and to deliver a speech. Talk about a bully pulpit—if we ever needed it, it is right now. He could have taken Hillary for her fiftieth birthday there rather than to Chicago. I would rather go to Geneva than Chicago in November. [laughter] That would have signaled that the GATT, now the WTO, has been a great success, a great success for everybody.

Porges: Let's return to the original question: Is GATT dead? Well, of course, it is dead. GATT 1947 was consciously killed off by the negotiators of the WTO. The European Community hated the protocol for the provisional application because they couldn't use it, so they killed that. They killed the Section 22 waiver because they hated that. As one of a number of symbolic acts associated with founding a new order, we killed the 1947 GATT partly to get rid of the free riders and to force everyone to enter the WTO regime, where, unlike the GATT, every country that belongs to the WTO has to have a schedule of tariff concessions and has to have a schedule of services concessions.

So the GATT is dead, but as you see, it is very, very much alive still. I listened to the accounts of the early years, and I too am struck by great diffusion that has occurred in the decision making of this organization and even in the life of the organization today as compared to the original GATT. It is true that real decisions are still made in small rooms but I think there are more people in those small rooms than there used to be.

It is partly because the developing countries got thoroughly worked over by the World Bank and the IMF. They had to open their trading regimes, and as a result they decided to go out and pay to get some trade concessions in the Uruguay Round.

There have been 104 complaints filed under the WTO dispute settlement regime since January 1, 1995. This compares to a total of 300 reported complaints in the fifty years of the GATT, so the WTO is catching up to the GATT at a rapid clip. Of the 104, 25 were started in 1995, 40 in 1996, and 44 so far this year. The pace is accelerating. Of the 104, 34 have been brought by developing countries—totally unheard of. It is very unusual that a developing country would bother suing anybody under the old GATT. And 42 of the 104 have been brought against developing countries. The Argentines did a ceiling binding, which they violated, and we sued them. I think that we expect to win and we expect that decision to stick. I think that is a real change. The Argentine private sector is going to have to live with the reality that they just can't go to their government when they have an import problem and get it fixed. So, the WTO has brought real change.

In the end I am really struck by the power of a single very corny word, *dreams.* This is a story in which believing it so has made it so. Enough people got together who really believed this would work, and it worked. Dispute settlement has gone in fifty years from a kind of group counseling effort at times to a really effective sanctions regime, a collective sanctions regime. Because the people who set this regime somehow set up the regime that accumulated a store of value in accumulated concessions that could be turned off by the contracting parties acting together. But what has happened is [that] somehow people have done the right things. The trade flows that they started have been able to change the political climate. Senator Millikin is also dead, along with GATT 1947. The GATT lives on, much more than Millikin does. Instead of Millikin and the mindless people who were his supporters, you have a vast business community which is now pushing for fast-track [authority to conduct negotiations] and pushing for trade liberalization because they depend on world markets. So, this is the world that the GATT has built. No, it is not dead.

Eckes: I want to thank the panelists for an excellent discussion. We have learned a great deal from them. Will the GATT system, and the WTO, endure for another fifty years? Perhaps the ITC Historical Society can revisit this discussion at the appropriate time. Hopefully, all of us will be available to participate in that session.

✧ CHAPTER THREE

The Kennedy Round Reconsidered

Participants: Francis M. Bator (White House), Herbert Blackman (Department of Labor), W. Michael Blumenthal (STR-Geneva), I. M. Destler (University of Maryland), Steve Dryden (*Bloomberg Financial News;* author), Theodore R. Gates (STR), Joseph A. Greenwald (Department of State), William T. Hart (Tariff Commission), Irwin R. Hedges (STR-Agriculture), William B. Kelly (Department of Commerce), Jeffrey Lang (USTR), James H. Lewis (Department of State), Harald Malmgren (STR), Robert L. McNeill (Department of Commerce), Bernard Norwood (STR), Gardner Patterson (GATT), Ernest Preeg (STR), John B. Rehm (STR), William M. Roth (STR), John A. Schnittker (Department of Agriculture), Thomas Zeiler (University of Colorado) This session took place May 5, 1997, at the U.S. International Trade Commission. The moderator was Alfred E. Eckes.

Alfred Eckes: Thirty years ago, on May 5, 1967, the front page of the *Washington Post* carried pictures of a new Apple Blossom queen and of U.S. Marines battling for Hill 881 in Vietnam. Buried on the business page was a headline about today's topic: "Bargaining Nears Climax: Kennedy Round Negotiators Hint of Tariff Compromises." Readers of the *New York Times* found a similar story back on the business page: "Tariff Talks Enter Last Phase: Some Optimism Voiced." That story also indicated that the Kennedy Round tariff talks had entered a final phase of nonstop negotiations. Over succeeding days the Kennedy Round would move from the business pages to the front pages. On Tuesday, May 16, the trade story dominated front-page headlines: "Kennedy Round Succeeds: 50 Nations To Cut Tariffs, Liberalizing World Trade."[1]

Today we revisit the famous Kennedy Round with a number of individuals prominently involved in the negotiations. Our panel also includes several scholars who have had an opportunity to examine the archival records and other sources, and to write about the Kennedy Round. Our discussion here will provide an indispensable supplement to written records when future generations of scholars and trade policy officials reexamine these events.

At the beginning we propose to consider as a panel the key issues and events in the Kennedy Round, and have a discussion among our participants. Later in the session we will have several short presentations from Ambassadors Roth and Blumenthal, as well as retrospective comment from Jeff Lang, the deputy U.S. trade representative. Afterward, we will attempt to assess the overall significance of the Kennedy Round for current and future policymakers.

Perhaps the proper place to initiate our discussion is with the prenegotiation phase. The Dillon Round of multilateral trade negotiations ended in 1962, but soon afterward the U.S. launched another round. What drove U.S. enthusiasm for another multilateral round and, from the vantage point of today, how do you assess those concerns?

Bernard Norwood: There was strong motivation for the Kennedy Round. The environment was perhaps discouraging, but the U.S. government never became discouraged enough to refrain from the proposed negotiations. The formation of the European Common Market raised U.S. concern that the [six-member] Community might become restrictive, and we wanted to have an influence on its common external tariff. In the Dillon Round [1961-62], Congress had given the president rather meager tariff-cutting authority compared to the steep cuts authorized in the early years of the trade agreements program. The Dillon Round also kept U.S. rights with regard to agricultural issues open for later resolution.

Another important development was the European Free Trade Association [EFTA]—involving the United Kingdom, among other European countries. The U.K. had an interest in joining the Common Market, and the United States was interested in making sure that such entry would not have restrictive effects on the U.S. or the rest of the world. In writing the Trade Expansion Act, Congress authorized removal of all tariffs on those commodities for which the U.S. and the European Community accounted for at least 80 percent of world trade.

Another issue involved Japan. During the period when John Foster Dulles was secretary of state [1953–59], the U.S. had promoted bilateral negotiations within the General Agreement on Tariffs and Trade . . . to bring Japan into the world trading community. Additionally, there was a U.S. concern about the plight of the less developed countries. The U.S. had a keen interest in promoting the economic advancement and industrialization of developing countries. Another round of negotiations might promote those goals.

Agriculture was a persistent problem in negotiations, not just with the EEC [European Economic Community] but with other countries as well.

There was another long-standing concern at the time the Trade Expansion Act of 1962 was passed, namely, that if you don't negotiate, you lose momentum and domestic and international protectionist forces will arise. The best way of deflecting some of those pressures is to undertake early negotiations. During negotiations, you can always say you cannot take restrictive action because it would disrupt negotiations.

Often the negotiations are looked at from a trade and economic point of view. But, the U.S. interest was much broader than that. Looking back at what President Kennedy told Governor Herter, the first special trade negotiator, in November of 1962, he said, "As you know, I accorded the Trade Expansion Act of 1962 the highest priority, requiring the nonpartisan support, and the unqualified commitment which must be provided legislation which affects the vital security interests of the United States both here and abroad. I requested and received authority from the Congress not only to pursue agreements on trade and tariffs which would accommodate our national needs for expanding markets and thereby contribute to our economic strength and growth, but also to create entirely new reciprocal trading arrangements which measurably contribute to the economic, political and military strength and solidarity of the free world. . . . Thus, the importance of this task and the scope of interest and endeavor of the Special Representative transcends particulars of negotiations on trade and tariff matters. This work goes to the very heart of the many policies and programs, domestic and foreign, which will help to shape the world environment in which the United States must maintain initiative, command respect, and provide leadership. . . .

"To this end, the Special Representative will necessarily be accorded a central role in the formulation of trade policy. He will be directly responsible for preparing the proposed objectives and strategies for negotiations and for directing those negotiations while they are in process. In a broader sense, he will become, along with the Secretaries of State and Commerce, one of the top policy officials of the United States Government in shaping and achieving our international objectives in the commercial, trade and economic fields."[2]

W. Michael Blumenthal: I would like to add some reflections. The real father of the Trade Expansion Act is not here, and that is George Ball. Without George Ball none of this would have happened. When he died [in May 1994] I had an opportunity to speak at his memorial service and I recalled that he was the father of all of this.

Let me reminisce. I came into the State Department in 1961 to be in charge of commodities, not trade. . . . I worked on coffee agreements, cocoa agreements, and lead-and-zinc study groups, and tin agreements, and all that good stuff. I had only the most marginal association with the trade area. The Office of Trade was headed by Len Weiss at the time.[3]

Ball ran his office like a lawyer's office. He had eight special assistants. But Ball liked to have lots of people around. He would often ask a few other young people to come and commune with him and he would listen to all of them and send us away and then he would draft his memorandum at three, four, or five o'clock in the morning. It was generally better than anything we had sent to him.

In 1961 and 1962 there was dismay in Mr. Ball's office about the extension of the reciprocal trade legislation. It was conventional thinking that there was no chance that the reciprocal trade legislation could be extended once again. Congress wouldn't do it. There was great fear that with the Common Market coming together and the Common Agricultural Policy taking shape, we would have great difficulty if we didn't do something.

Many memoranda were written but nobody had a very good operational idea. I happened to be present at a critical meeting that involved a consultant, Raymond Vernon, who had been in the State Department and later became a distinguished economist in Harvard University. At that meeting Vernon said, "George [Ball], if you can't go forward, you might as well make a big jump. Suggest something that nobody has every tried before. Quit fooling around with peril points and all that stuff. Just suggest 50-percent-across-the-board cuts." Maybe it had been rumored outside in the halls [of the State Department] previously, but Vernon put it forward in this way. And to his credit, George Ball picked it up immediately and said that we can have a political explanation for why this bold step must be done. It is the challenge of the Common Market. It [the single market] is coming together. The United States will be frozen out. That is the origin of the Trade Expansion Act and the particular authority that was proposed to Congress. I recall that meeting very, very clearly.

I had no idea that I would be involved in the negotiations. I went back to my cotton textiles that evening. [In passing the Trade Expansion Act] Congress said we will give you that authority, but not if the State Department is in charge. We don't trust the State Department. The State Department always sells us out to the foreigners. That's how STR [Special Trade Representative] was created in the spring of 1963. Governor Herter was brought in. A gentleman by the name of Bill Gossett came in as his deputy. I was sent . . . to the preparatory meeting before a ministerial meeting in May 1963. It was agreed that a State Department officer could do that since it was a preparatory meeting. I was already working for Governor Herter but I still had my State Department hat on.

The main ministerial meeting set the framework for what was negotiated later. It was a very difficult meeting. Governor Herter went; Mr. Gossett went. Many of us went. Subsequently, Mr. Gossett resigned, and Governor Herter asked me to become his deputy.

Eckes: John Rehm, could you tell us about the origins of the Trade Expansion Act and whether it went far enough to provide the mandate for Kennedy Round negotiations, particularly on the nontariff issues?

John Rehm: I would agree with Ambassador Blumenthal about George Ball's role. But I want to give credit to Wilbur Mills, chairman of the House Ways and Means Committee. He is remembered by many for his episode in the Tidal Basin, but he was one of the finest members of Congress that I have ever worked with.[4] He was intelligent and balanced. In those days, the chairman of the Ways and Means Committee had awesome authority. By carrying Democrats along with him, he could override Republicans. . . . Mills was very solidly behind us, very much supportive of the New Deal trade liberalization program.

There was one issue where Chairman Mills became more and more determined, more and more adamant. As Mike Blumenthal has already said, he, and perhaps most of the Congress, had accepted the argument, valid or otherwise, that the State Department had disproportionate influence over the conduct of trade negotiations. How deeply personally he believed that, I don't know. But he certainly saw some change as politically necessary. He did not want to take the bill to the floor without some institutional change. That led him to propose the idea [for STR], which may originally have been Mike Rashish's notion.[5]

Chairman Mills was prepared to take the bill to the floor of the House largely as we sent it up to him, but only if there was to be a new Office of the Special Trade Representative reporting not to the secretary of state but to the president himself. That set off a bitter battle within the executive branch. Some arguing that of course you have to go along with the chairman in order to move the bill. The State Department and particularly George

Ball . . . argued that our trade policy was a subset of our foreign policy. . . . Ball lost. President Kennedy accepted the idea of a special trade representative reporting directly to the president. When the bill went over to the Senate, we were confronted with a series of Bush amendments, involving the father of President George H. W. Bush [Senator Prescott Bush (R-Conn.)]. We beat those. But I want to stress that Wilbur Mills played a major role in enacting the legislation.

Looking back as to whether the Trade Expansion Act of 1962 gave adequate authority to negotiate on nontariff barriers, the basic delegation of authority in the Trade Expansion Act of 1962 (similar to that in the original 1934 legislation) was to "proclaim such modification or continuance of any existing duty or other import restriction." Read literally, the phrase "or other import restriction" could have embraced any number of nontariff barriers and thereby give[n] the president unforeseen and unprecedented authority to amend a range of U.S. laws that imposed import restrictions of one kind or another, including American selling price and antidumping duties.

However, for political reasons—with which I agreed—such a sweeping interpretation of the president's authority would have been too much for the Congress to accept. Thus, in response to your second question, I would say that the legal authority to deal with nontariff barriers was more than adequate. We simply used it more conservatively. For political reasons, it was decided to make American selling price the subject of a separate agreement which was submitted to the Congress for implementing legislation. With respect to the antidumping code, we argued—unsuccessfully—that it was consistent with existing law and did not require implementing legislation.

John Schnittker: The farm community in the early 1960s was not tuned in to trade but it was very enthusiastic about taking trade out of the State Department and therefore supported the establishment of STR. The native suspicion of the agricultural community goes back a long ways. In the 1920s and 1930s, agriculture produced surpluses but there was very little world market. The farmer's orientation toward exports was very limited in the 1920s and 1930s. There just wasn't anything there. You had things to sell but people wouldn't buy much. Then came World War II and afterward the U.S. role in feeding the world. Thus, in the late 1940s and 1950s agriculture became oriented to exports, although much of this was not commercial trade. In the late 1950s other countries began to recover, and postwar aid began a transition to trade. That occurred near the beginning of the Kennedy Round.

Two other comments about the agricultural policies of that time. The European Community was being formed and the European Community was on a bad track as far as agricultural policy was concerned. For the community was trying to organize agriculture around a system of very high support prices, which seemed certain to increase production and therefore to reduce trade. At the same time the U.S. was at a standstill in agricultural policy. Secretary of Agriculture Orville Freeman, like the good liberal Democrat that he was, wanted to raise price supports, wanted to increase farm spending, but having done so on one or two commodities, immediately was confronted with budget problems. The price supports induced more production. That was the policy status and the frame of mind of the farm community as the Kennedy Round began.

I. M. Destler: I have a question about the Trade Expansion Act of 1962. Looking back, one is impressed with how lean this bill was, and how few congressional appendages, other than STR, were attached. Is the simple answer two words—Wilbur Mills—or is it the brilliance of administration lobbying, or were there some important reasons why Congress did not get into the very extensive rewriting of U.S. trade law that occurred in 1974 and thereafter?

Rehm: Just as George Ball looms over this whole effort in the executive branch, so does Wilbur Mills. . . . We tend to forget that this was still an era when the chairmen of congressional committees were very powerful. Mills's power was also based on an amazing intellect. I can recall a markup on a terribly technical issue, and we were privileged to attend the markup so we could see the process work. The discussion went back and forth between legislative and executive branch officials among members of the committee for forty-five minutes to an hour. Mills had to sit back and gavel. Now and then he would put his gavel down and he would summarize that very technical, complex debate with absolute brilliance. I really think his personal stature played a role. He was also famous for being very cautious in taking a bill to the floor of the House. While still in committee, he took great pains to assure that it would have the support of a clear majority of the members of the House.

He was determined not to lose on the House floor. He thought he had a winner with the plan to create the Office of the Special Trade Representative. When it came to the Senate side, our bill was managed by Senator [Robert] Kerr of Oklahoma, a very wily and shrewd man, and he warned us that Senator Bush had amendments lying in waiting that would have crippled the bill. Bush proposed several amendments, and each was, as I recall, decisively defeated. Bush then gave up and, from that point on, the bill sailed through the Senate essentially unscathed.

Blumenthal: I think it is very true that without Wilbur Mills we would never have gotten this negotiating authority, and without George Ball's initial political calculation we would not have been where we were either. By suggesting something entirely different, an across-the-board cut with a minimum of exceptions, you would catch the usual nay-sayers in congressional trade debates off base. That was the political judgment that was made, and it shifted the whole nature of the campaign. And, with the positive political argument that this would be a way to deal with the EEC's Common Agricultural Policy, the argument had added appeal. This made it somewhat easier for Mr. Mills, and those who were fighting this bill through Congress, to keep the problems to a minimum.

Irwin Hedges: I want to add a footnote to the eulogy to Mr. Mills. He not only was involved in the creation of the legislation but he followed it intimately throughout the negotiations process. I met with him on numerous occasions and in various committees where he arbitrated problems of agricultural negotiations. One Friday afternoon a group of us met in his office—the negotiators and industry representatives. It was an issue of thorny substance and we couldn't reach agreement in his office that afternoon.

He closed the meeting by saying, I want you to spend the weekend and come back with a solution on Monday morning. Well, the industry group and ourselves spent ten or twelve hours on Saturday and Sunday, and we did come back Monday morning with a solution which was acceptable for presentation to Wilbur Mills.

Herbert Blackman: Another important factor in the legislation involved labor unions. At that time the labor movement was still relatively friendly to international trade, except perhaps for the textile area, which the cotton agreements took care of. Inclusion of the adjustment assistance provisions was meant to bring the labor movement along. It is true that these provisions didn't work for a long time, but at that time the unions supported the legislation.

Thomas Zeiler: Did anyone in the State Department fight the creation of the Special Trade Representative? If many from the State Department served in STR did this really represent a significant change?

Blumenthal: I want to answer the previous question and this one as well. The State Department was bureaucratically split between two different groups. The trade people were what some people refer to as GATT theologians. They looked at things in historical terms, based on their experiences and the rules of the GATT. They were the defenders of the GATT, and its representatives, for a long, long time.

You have to remember that George Ball was a Europeanist first and foremost. Trade to him was important in this context primarily because it was a critical component of our relationship with the European Economic Community, which was still a tender creation in the process of being developed. He knew we had to defend our interests, but at the same time he thought how the Community developed was infinitely more important than what we did on canned hams. But to other people canned ham was very, very important. So the tension between what became STR and the State Department was complicated by internal divisions within the State Department. But, the Europeanists—with Mr. Ball on the seventh floor—were in control. Incidentally, one of the reasons why Ambassador [Joseph] Greenwald was called back to take over that office as office director and deputy assistant secretary was exactly because he was knowledgeable on trade matters but also part of the Europeanist Mafia in the State Department. He came to take that job because George Ball thought there would be less bureaucratic infighting in the State Department if someone like Joe were running the department, and that is exactly what happened.

Before Francis Bator came to the White House, George Ball dealt somewhat with Carl Kaysen, and that was about it. Obviously, I am not privy to how much briefing Carl Kaysen gave to Mac Bundy but I believe that the president was only involved to the extent that textiles were taken care of.[6] That was a condition precedent. We had to have something on textiles. That is why there was the one-year agreement and the promise of a five-year agreement, because we could not have the support—he had promised it in the campaign—of the New England delegation and the Southerners without the textile agreement.

Along the line the chicken question came up. That had a lot to do with Wilbur Mills. We had a situation where both the chairman of the Ways and Means Committee [Wilbur Mills] and the chairman of Senate Foreign Relations [William Fulbright] were from Arkansas, and so chickens became an absolutely critical item. I should know, I was the commanding general of the "chicken war," which occurred a little later. That's how we kept the support of Wilbur Mills, because we fought for chickens. If we had not fought vigorously on chickens, we would have lost him.

Rehm: It is my understanding and recollection that once President Kennedy made the go-ahead decision, it then became largely, if not wholly, a matter of delegating key functions. . . . A banker from Philadelphia, Howard Petersen, came on, and it was his task to coordinate the lobbying operation with Congress and with the interests outside of Congress. Internally, Secretary of Commerce [Luther] Hodges was made head of the interagency group that steered the legislation through the House and the Senate. My impression is that once Kennedy said yes, the matter left the White House and devolved to these two individuals in particular.

Francis Bator: John [Rehm], was there a fight within the executive branch before the president made his decision, or was the recommendation pretty unanimous across the major executive departments?

Rehm: My recollection is that there was no great dispute, and Ball carried the day.

Blumenthal: He carried the day, but there were disputes on what reservations should be made. I believe Secretary Hodges [Commerce], in particular, and Secretary [Orville] Freeman [Agriculture] were in general support, but were very, very cautious. What exactly was meant by 50-percent-across-the-board tariff cuts, and how would agriculture be included? These were not easy questions. The whole cabinet was not immediately in favor. I believe in particular that Secretary Hodges was concerned about the lowering of protection in the United States.

Robert McNeill: Secretary Hodges's name came up and since I was his subordinate, I would like to offer an anecdote about the establishment of the Office of the Special Trade Representative. During the course of putting the Trade Expansion Act together, we had considerable discussion about the establishment of the trade representative's office. At one point Secretary Hodges called us all in—the undersecretaries, assistant secretaries, and myself—to discuss the matter. The undersecretary made a recommendation that Secretary Hodges call the president and suggest that the authority for administering the Trade Expansion Act be legislatively given to the secretary of commerce. Secretary Hodges looked at those in the room and said, "What do you gentlemen think?" They all said, "Gee, that is a great idea." And the secretary asked me what I thought. I had just recently joined him from the staff of the Bureau of the Budget. I told him that I thought that it was totally inappropriate for the secretary of commerce to chair and administer the authorities of the Trade Expansion Act because I thought the interests involved in that act transcended the viewpoint of a department that represented the business community's interest in the president's cabinet. I made that comment—and there was absolute shock on the part of everybody. I wished I had wings and could have flown out that window and escaped. The secretary was shocked. Then he looked at me and he smiled nicely and said, "Bob is right. I agree." That was my personal contribution to avoiding a fight from the Commerce Department side on the chairmanship and administering authority of the Trade Expansion Act.

It is true that the business community generally had an abiding interest in the formation of the Common Market and lowering the barriers that the common external tariff posed to American exporters. Although the business community was generally friendly to the authorities of the Trade Expansion Act, there was a lot of divisiveness. Mike [Blumenthal] will particularly remember an assistant secretary named Hickman Price, who was responsible within the Commerce Department for domestic affairs and textiles. I can recall a meeting where he said, instead of 50-percent tariff-cutting authority we should go 100 percent. We really should be as bold as George Ball wants us to be, he said, except that the cuts should not apply to all classes of products, particularly to textiles. In our department we agreed that the 50-percent cut, applicable to all classes of products, made more sense.

Let me offer another comment about Wilbur Mills. In those days the congressional committees had very few subcommittees. In particular, the Ways and Means Committee had no subcommittee. The Ways and Means Committee dealt with taxes as a committee, with trade as a committee, and with other areas of its responsibility as a full committee. The Ways and Means Committee, in addition to having substantive control over the trade area, in those days was also what was called the Committee on Committees. That meant that for every assignment of a congressman to a committee, that assignment was granted by, and approved by, the House Ways and Means Committee. So in addition to being a legislative committee, it was also the committee to which all 435 congressmen owed their committee assignments. You can imagine that with such broader authority Wilbur Mills had friends throughout the House of Representatives and throughout all the committees. In those days dealing with Congress on trade matters was very simple. If you could get Mr. Mills on an issue, you in effect had the House of Representatives, and that in fact is what happened with the Trade Expansion Act. I think the vote was 300 for and 150 opposed. If you had Mr. Mills, and Mr. [John] Byrnes, the Republican minority senior member, you in effect had the Congress. So when Mr. Mills agreed with the viewpoint of the president, as expressed through George Ball and others, that there was a political imperative in joining with the Common Market to have a global reduction of tariffs, the fight was in very large part won.

Norwood: The concern that Tom Zeiler referred to—the position of the Department of State in the Office of the Special Trade Representative—was quite sensitive. It has a deeper background. Since its creation in the early 1930s, the trade agreements program had been in the hands of an interagency committee, which was not a regular interagency committee. The Trade Agreements Committee had been set up by executive order. The committee itself was given responsibilities for administering the reciprocal trade agreements program. It even got to the point after a change in administration where one of the senior officials, who was serving as a chair or vice chair of that committee before STR, resented the intrusion of the secretary of state and objected to the secretary's trying to give instructions to the Trade Agreements Committee. The committee was chaired by a senior-working-level member of the Department of State, and it considered itself as having full authority, even to the point where it could ignore the instructions of the secretary of state.

When the Kennedy transition took place, implementing the legislation as John Rehm has described, the Trade Staff Committee was the immediate successor of the Trade Agreements Committee. This committee was part of a new structure, and reflected a totally different concept. The Trade Staff Committee was senior working level, and carried on from the Trade Agreements Committee in that sense. There was another level—Trade Executive Committee—above that, and then a cabinet-level committee above that one. Governor Herter considered that all those committees were advisory to him. They could have voted unanimously on something, and they could be overruled. The special trade representative, or even the deputy special trade representative, could overrule them.

I was quite aware of the sensitivity that some of the people referred to. As the first chair of the Trade Staff Committee, I moved about rather cautiously. I listened to all the members of the committee, and did so not in the order in which they are ordinarily referred to in the government manual—the order of their creation under the U.S. Constitution—State, Treasury, and down the line—but I did so alphabetically. I was also careful to choose staff from different departments. When it came to finding a deputy, since the committee had gotten very busy, I did select someone from another agency—Al Powers from the Department of Commerce. Those decisions reflected the sensitivity. Also, during the period of its operation, I tried very carefully to be quite balanced, not to give preference to any agency. I don't think anyone—to my face anyway—accused me of being biased. I would say that we drew heavily on people from State and the Foreign Service, especially when we were building up the delegation [for the Kennedy Round negotiations]. There is a very sensitive background to STR's creation: the role of State and Commerce in the management of the trade agreements program.

Bator: A story that ought to go into the record bears on George Ball's priorities. The Department of State's position in relation to our relations with the Common Market and the EEC played a major role in interdepartmental debates on strategy in the period from 1964 to 1967. George Ball led a small delegation in March 1961 to Bonn, Brussels, Paris, and London. The main purpose was to try and get the Europeans to increase their aid levels to help us push the Congress harder on getting the foreign assistance act back through after creating the Agency for International Development. I was then teaching at MIT, but he asked me to come down, and I spent six weeks working for him on aid-related matters. He asked me to go along. The trip ended in London, and I recall our meeting at the Board of Trade. Ted Heath was Lord Privy Seal, and we had a meeting in his conference room. He was in charge, and George Ball on our side. David Bruce was the ambassador. Bob Schaetzel, Mike Rashish, and I were there. There was a division bell, so Heath had to leave. Frank Lee, the permanent undersecretary, took the chair.

He turned to George across the table, gave him a hard look, and said, "George, is it the policy of the new administration that we join Europe?"

I saw a lot of George Ball subsequently, and it is one of the few occasions when I saw him turn a little green. But, with only a moment's hesitation, he said: "Yes, that is our view." The meeting ended and we left. George got in the back seat of the Cadillac, and Schaetzel and I were sitting on the jump seat. The undersecretary of state for economic affairs said, "You know, I have never spoken to the president about this. And I have never spoken to Dean [Rusk], the secretary of state, about this. Was it OK?" The point is that priority was very clear in George Ball's head, and it came later to powerfully influence the State Department position on the set of arguments that we had in 1964, 1965, 1966, and 1967 about how to proceed.

Eckes: Let's turn now to a discussion of the Kennedy Round negotiations. It is my impression that many governments were far less interested than the United States in entering a new round of multilateral negotiations. Do any of you recall why other governments were so cool to another round of GATT negotiations?

Blumenthal: I had the task of leading the discussions preparatory to the May 1963 ministerial meeting at which the governor and Mr. Gossett appeared with a large and messy delegation. There were at least three or four cabinet officers present, and all of their minions, assistants, and briefcase carriers. I would say the reaction of the foreign governments was what you would have expected at the time. The Europeans were stunned. They did not expect the United States ever to have this kind of negotiating authority. Then they began to quibble and argue, to say, Well it sounds good but I guess you will have lots of exceptions, so it won't mean very much. There was a division within the six countries of the Common Market because the Germans and the Dutch, traditionally low-protection, open-market countries, thought that was a great idea. The French, usually quite protectionist, were quite, quite nervous. So it was quite difficult for the Common Market, which was the story of our lives for the next four years, to make any kind of decision.

The EFTA [European Free Trade Association] countries generally welcomed it, because they saw it as a way to get better access to all the markets. The agriculture-exporting countries generally welcomed it, because we said agriculture absolutely had to be included, and they believed it. The Japanese basically went along, hoping for even more access to the developed-country markets for their products. In those days the Japanese were still important exporters of textiles. Things have changed. They were one of our problems in the cotton textile negotiations. So I would say the Europeans were somewhat mixed. Some more protectionist countries led by the French didn't really believe us. They were shocked when they found out we really meant it. Some countries, primarily the nonprotectionist ones, enthusiastically supported it. And others hoped to pick something up without giving too much.

Gardner Patterson: On this last point I think one of the great problems of the European Community was the necessity of reaching a set position—to get one position. In Geneva that was very hard for them to do, because there had to be a lot of trade-offs, and if you were going to get something on dairy products you had to pay in some other way. So you had a lot of internal negotiations within the Community itself before they could reach a position. And often that position would be the least common denominator.

Schnittker: Following up on what Gardner said, I recall an early meeting in 1963-1964 of the grains and meats negotiating group. The Community was represented, but so were the six countries. The Community representative was very anxious not to state anything in any way that would upset the representatives of the six member countries sitting behind him. So it was not only difficult to make a decision but even to make a statement.

Norwood: Some of the laggards haven't been mentioned. The first consultation Governor Herter had outside the country was with Japan. I accompanied him to Tokyo in April 1963 and we met with the entire Japanese government—Mr. Ikeda, the prime minister, and on down. They had mixed views. They were a bit reluctant. They were still recovering from World War II, they reminded us, and they couldn't afford to do certain things. They didn't want to be obstreperous. After all, it was the United States which had brought them along. So they told us about all the problems that they had, but said they weren't opposed. They were prepared to go along, but were quite apprehensive.

A week after that, we flew up to Ottawa to meet with the Canadian government and give them encouragement. They had some interest, but were worried about renegotiating internally their machinery tariff. That was a big problem for them, and they had some other concerns too. The big problem we faced in Ottawa was that we landed there days after the new government came into power. We were pleased to see one of our GATT working stiffs now a member of Parliament. That was Mitchell Sharpe, who became minister of trade in that government and later the foreign minister. We had a great discussion, but we had to cut it off, because some of these members of the new government hadn't met each other. They had been out on the hustings and this was the first occasion to meet each other.

So in these two cases, the others were willing to go along, but with some reluctance. It was the U.S. which was pulling everyone. The United States was the only country that was promoting this negotiation. Others might be interested, or might not, but it was the U.S. initiative.

Eckes: What was the attitude of the developing countries?

Schnittker: The developing countries, being heavily agricultural, were generally in favor but also suspicious because it was being run by the rich countries.

Joseph Greenwald: They believed in special and differential treatment. They figured it would be a free ride and they wouldn't have to pay anything.

Blumenthal: I can summarize it: What will you give us? We need it, but of course we can't pay.

Schnittker: As a footnote, I recall that at one point in the grains talk, Argentina and Australia wanted to be developing countries as well, so as to have special exceptions, even though by that time they were relatively rich countries.

Norwood: There was a group of seventy-seven less developed countries in the UN, moving as they preferred through the UN Conference on Trade and Development to get special benefits.

They were organized, so they could operate largely as a coalition in demanding things from developed countries in the Kennedy Round.

Ernest Preeg: My recollection is that Canada was not prepared to accept the 50-percent-across-the-board [formula]. In their own way they always wanted special and differential treatment. At the real crux of the 50-percent-across-the-board negotiation was an inner circle composed of Japan, the United Kingdom, the U.S., and the European Community. This group was quite different from recent years. The so-called Quad no longer includes the U.K., but it does Canada. Canada got into the inner group because Canadians changed their approach to support equal treatment.

Blumenthal: Ernie Preeg is absolutely right. Someone would have to go back to the basic document—the ministerial agreement of May 1963. I think there is a special paragraph in there for Canada. Canada was insistent that they had to have special rules.

Norwood: I think it is misleading to phrase it as Ernie did. Someone might get the impression that Canada was not prepared to make big cuts. To the extent that they were prepared to go into negotiations, they were saying they'll make cuts. They couldn't accept the linear rule. . . . They had to have their own negotiating technique.

Patterson: The cereals arrangement raised one of the more bizarre incidents in the Kennedy Round. The countries had great difficulty reaching a memorandum of understanding about cereals. . . . A meeting was held in Wyndham White's office, and a message came over from UNCTAD, a personal message from Raul Prebisch, the director general at that time. He said, It has come to my attention that GATT is negotiating an agreement on cereals; I wish to remind the members of GATT that under UN Resolution so-and-so, governments have agreed that all commodity agreements shall be negotiated in the UNCTAD. Somebody said that's right. Somebody else said that's what happens when the State Department attends international meetings, since only the State Department was represented in UNCTAD. What should we do? Finally the Japanese ambassador, who had been very quiet, and not very helpful, said, Why don't we pretend we never got the letter. That broke up the meeting.

Eckes: You have raised the agricultural negotiations. Perhaps this would be a good time to pursue that issue. What did the U.S. want? In retrospect, did we place undue emphasis on the willingness of other countries to offer significant concessions?

Hedges: Let me make a general statement. With respect to the organization of STR, there was never any support in the Agriculture Department for the secretary of commerce, or any other cabinet officer, having that responsibility. The Department of Agriculture was one of the major supporters of an independent STR. The Department of Agriculture did insist that agriculture be included in the negotiations, but I found one of my parallel responsibilities, when I got to STR, in addition to working in my main field of getting concessions in agriculture, was to restrain the public relations people at STR from putting excessively strong statements in the speeches of the administrator about the necessity of agriculture being included in the negotiations. Those of us working in agriculture were realistic from the beginning that the possibilities of carrying out extensive negotiations in agriculture were very limited.

Let me read very briefly from a paper I have here dated 1964, which states the U.S. delegation's position concerning the proposal of the European Community for agricultural negotiations: "The EEC has made a proposal to form the basis of agricultural negotiations, the fundamental element of which is the binding of margins of support above a fixed reference price. The United States cannot accept the Community's proposal as a basis of negotiations because it not only fails to provide for reductions in existing trade barriers but would introduce new restrictions and increase protection." That is essentially the Common Agricultural Policy, which had not yet evolved. The EEC was not in a position to negotiate meaningfully on agricultural restrictions.

Subsequently there was some criticism that we should have taken as a negotiating position the EEC proposal to freeze their margins of support above fixed prices. We carefully and fully examined that at the time. In the first place it was only for three years and in the second it was so adorned by restrictions, limitations, and other provisions as to be utterly meaningless in trade terms. Also, at that time the United Kingdom was not able to negotiate meaningfully on agriculture. They had not yet made their decision to join the Common Market. They realized that there would be a major problem in reconciling their domestic policies with the Common Agricultural Policy.

The United States was in an equally difficult position. In essence, what we recognized at that time was that meaningful agricultural negotiations in the Kennedy Round would involve changes in domestic agricultural price supports and programs. The United States was no more in a position to negotiate internationally on that than any other country. Indeed, we took the position at that time that domestic payments to farmers were not relevant to agricultural trade, a position which personally I think is absurd. We were not in a position to negotiate on things like that or on the impact of conservation and other payments affecting agricultural production.

Having said all that, I do think that we had modest success in the agricultural negotiations. It was limited, but there were some things that really were improved. I have a letter here that I received from the National Canners' Association citing the benefits they gained in the Kennedy Round and also a personal letter that I received thanking me for my efforts and our success in that field.

The other major agricultural concern in the Kennedy Round was grains. In this we were unable to [bargain] successfully. . . . We took a position until the final negotiating sessions that there would be no Kennedy Round concluded without meaningful access for the United States against the restrictive grain import regulation that both the United Kingdom and the EEC had. It fell to my lot at one of the last plenary sessions to recommend to Governor Herter and to Bill Roth, Mike Blumenthal, that we simply drop that provision because it was obvious we couldn't fulfill it. Wyndham White and some of our colleagues were very stunned when we dropped that position. But even in grains we went ahead and negotiated a so-called grains agreement. I can immodestly say that I was thanked afterwards by some of the major individuals in the grain trade for having done nothing to restrain U.S. freedom of action with that agreement. [laughter] I left it to Hal Malmgren to finish that agreement, which was signed in July 1967 in Rome.

There was one important thing that we did accomplish in the grains agreement. We got the EEC and other grain traders to make contributions to the world food program. That not only had humanitarian benefits but it relieved some of the pressure on commercial markets.

As an anecdote to show how domestic agricultural policies restricted opportunities, we had a plenary session at which Commissioner [Jean] Rey, the spokesman for the EEC, proposed that the U.S. reduce import restrictions on butter. Well, at that time both the EEC and the U.S. had accumulated enormous stocks of butter in their price support programs. There was a stunned silence on our side, and after a few seconds I asked the permission of our superiors to respond.

I said, "Commissioner Rey, at least in our country there is a certain prestige at times to using imported products. Now we both have surpluses in butter that we don't know what to do with. If it would help the European Community at all, perhaps we could arrange an equal trade pound for pound of butter, and each of us could advertise it as an imported product." After the laughter subsided, we moved on to other things and no other mention was made of it.

Schnittker: The strong statement that Irwin Hedges referred to, repeated by Governor Herter and others in 1963, 1964, and 1965, that there can be no final bargain unless there is liberalization in agriculture, became an important political rallying point for the farming community. Being in the Department of Agriculture, we had to take note of that political point. On at least two occasions in 1966 and 1967, toward the end of the Kennedy Round, I accompanied Secretary Freeman to the White House. Mike Blumenthal might have been called back from Geneva. Bill Roth was there. And we proposed as directly as we could that it was time to deliver for agriculture. It was time to bring the negotiations to a close, or at least to inform the world that there could be no final bargain on textiles or tariff cutting or whatever unless they were more forthcoming on agriculture, particularly by not raising their support levels so high. We always lost. And slowly the agricultural bargaining got whittled down, necessarily to the point Irwin Hedges has just described.

Eckes: Why did agriculture lose?

Bator: Speaking with precision and certainty about what was in President Johnson's head is difficult. To use Mac Bundy's phrase, he hated to be understood. Although I dealt very closely with him over a great range of issues in 1965, 1966, and 1967, there was always a problem of inference, of finding out what his priority was. It became very clear to me by the end of 1965 that he very much wanted a serious bargain in the Kennedy Round. He did not want the negotiations to fail. He was prepared to back away in the end from the U.S. commitment to a big bargain in agriculture, prepared to accept what we could get, in order make a big industrial bargain.[7]

William Roth: I think it incumbent on me to say just a few words. Listening to this discussion takes me back. When I came to STR in 1963, I didn't know very much about trade. All of you around the table instructed me. [laughter] I gradually began to learn the things we have been discussing here. How behind these arcane matters dealing with rather small items, like canned hams, lie rather large policy questions. When I came to STR the "chicken war" was in its final phase. I remember my only meeting with President Kennedy, a couple months before he was killed, with Governor Herter, Secretary Freeman, Secretary Rusk. Kennedy was studying some papers when I was introduced and grunted. Governor Herter explained the problems of the "chicken war," and Kennedy looked up and asked the question, "Is de Gaulle behind it?" [laughter]

Secretary Freeman said, "There is no question."

Secretary Rusk said, "I would doubt whether he was involved with chickens. He may be informed about it, but it is not part of his grand policy."

Governor Herter agreed with Secretary Freeman, and the result was that the U.S. stuck firm on chickens. It was adjudicated in Geneva. The U.S. was awarded compensation, and Bernie Norwood's committee carefully selected four items that would hurt France, the Netherlands, Germany, and nobody else. It was done with brilliant success. For Germany it was the minibuses, which they soon changed to trucks, and they came in anyhow. For France, it was cognac, but the higher the price the more you sell.

Behind all these things, there is a sweep of policy that is important. Rereading some of these marvelous old cables, we sound like small boys playing games, but these things were important.

I want to say one more thing more about the Office of STR. The issue of where trade policy should be made was argued before the office was established and has been argued ever since. Proposals are always appearing to give trade policy back to Commerce, or to place all the trade activities in a megatrade department. The approach stipulated in the Trade Expansion Act, a Special Trade Representative with a coordinating function, worked extremely well because the various interests were balanced. During negotiations everyone worked as a team. Thus, looking around this table, it is very much like the participation we had in Geneva during the final negotiations—about this size.

Mike and I were negotiating with Jean Rey and the Community. We couldn't get everybody in. Phil Trezise came up with Bob [McNeill] and did Canada. Greenwald did the U.K. Mike and I could just wash our hands until the ambassador from the U.K. called and said, "Can't you do something and get rid of that guy? [laughter] He is being much too difficult."

John [Schnittker] and Irwin [Hedges] did agriculture. John Rehm, you were in charge of the ASP [American selling price] negotiations, as I recall. That approach worked. I hope it does now. I know that STR has grown, but it remains relatively small.

Rehm: Speaking only for myself, I don't think any of my colleagues had any conception then about the significance of the creation of what was a tiny, tiny agency with no more than fifteen professionals and our reliance on other agencies. We were struggling to put something together. Even after the first four or five years, if we had all been polled, we would have been uncertain about the future of this office. I can recall vividly that in doing the budget we violated all the principles of an executive agency of the president, which is what we were. That principle being that any agency in the Executive Office of the President should be advisory only and have no so-called action responsibility. Here you had not only a coordinating group but one responsible for a major set of negotiations. But here we are in the 1990s, and I fully agree with Bill Roth, I think it has been a major success because it has permitted a balance of interests without going too far to the protection side or the liberal side. It has been a remarkably productive mechanism for coordinating, establishing, pursuing, and implementing U.S. foreign trade policy, and I say that having drafted those two executive orders. I am still astonished that it worked as well as it has.

McNeill: This is a comment on the importance of chickens. In the board room of each auto manufacturer should be a picture of a chicken. Let me tell you why. Ambassador Roth was just talking about the list of items we chose to retaliate against because the Europeans were not forthcoming and not living up to their GATT obligations. To get back at Germany we raised the duty on small trucks, almost exclusively manufactured by Volkswagen and exported to the U.S. market, and we snapped back the duty to about 25 percent. That is still the governing duty on imported small trucks. For those who follow the American automobile industry, well over half of the total production currently is in the category of trucks. That 25-percent duty is in substantial part responsible for the success of the American automakers in this area. I say in all seriousness, the number one legislative priority for the American automobile industry is to make certain that tariff is not changed by executive action or by legislative change. I mention this because when we talk about chickens, they truly are important.

Blumenthal: Could I just mention quickly two people who need to be mentioned. When we talk about the success of STR from its original beginnings and the success of the Kennedy Round, these two really deserve mention. I don't know who thought of Chris Herter as the first STR, that was a brilliant decision. . . .

Norwood: Mike Rashish took credit for that.

Blumenthal: It deserves praise, posthumous praise. It was a brilliant decision in my view, because it put firmly the stamp of bipartisanship on this trade effort. It was a very important thing. Chris Herter had been a secretary of state, a Republican, a governor, a distinguished member of Congress. There were lots of other names put forward. The choice of him was very, very important, even though his health was not the best. His brain was fine. He knew exactly what it was about. I asked him once at lunch, Why did you do this governor? You have done all these things. Why did you go into trade? This is peanuts compared to what you have done. He said, "Mike, because I have always known that there is more international politics wrapped up in these trade matters than most people realize."

The second person who had much to do with the success of the Kennedy Round was, until the last weeks (because he didn't do too well in the last weeks), was Wyndham White. We were fortunate to have a very good director general of the GATT. Wyndham was a towering figure in the trade field. I don't know what we would do without him during critical periods. He was blessed with a very competent staff, particularly Finn Gundelach and Gardner [Patterson]. Internally there may have been tensions at times, for Wyndham White was a difficult person, but Wyndham White really had an authority in the trade world that has never been matched since. That had a lot to do with keeping us on an even keel. Those two people are important. I say until the very end because in some strange way, in the very last two or three weeks of the Kennedy Round, Wyndham White was at his wit's end. I don't know for what reason. It was really Finn Gundelach in my view, and I personally was present, who helped in the final nights—the last several nights when we worked all through the night, to put the agreement together. Wyndham White just couldn't do it any more. He was at the end of his rope. But through four years of negotiations, without him, I don't know whether we would have succeeded. It would have been much more difficult.

Question from audience: I am Amy Porges, current staff of USTR. I have three large questions, which vary between the big picture and the technical. First, I think everyone would love to hear more about the nontariff agenda in the Kennedy Round, particularly the antidumping code. I understand there was also work done on procurement, valuation, customs issues. How was it that dumping in the end floated up as the one subject that people took on? How was this code developed? I understand that the earliest proposals were from the U.K. Why was the U.K. pushing this? We would love to hear more.

Second, another pre-Kennedy Round issue. When the EC was formed, they took an equal average of the tariffs, of the constituent customs territories, and the result was that tariffs went up a lot on some products—particularly tropical products. At the same time, on those tropical products the Community had preferences for the former colonies, which meant that Latin America was one of the big losers when the EC was formed. How was this sorted out within the State Department? Were the Europeanists simply dominant, or wasn't there anyone speaking up for our traditional friends in Latin America?

Third question: formula tariff cutting. Where did formula tariff cutting come from? I have heard that the first tariff cuts that were actually implemented came as part of the EC's process of getting to the common external tariff, and the earliest formula proposals were in the Dillon Round. Was this the EC's idea? Was it Ray Vernon's idea? Where did it come from?

A final stunningly technical question is, Who invented the floating INR?

Eckes: For the benefit of the audience, what is the floating INR?

Porges: The floating INR was invented in the Kennedy Round to deal with the whole issue of what happens to the initial negotiating right, the right to be consulted and the right to be paid if the tariff has ever been negotiated. Traditionally, in the world of principal supplier, the principal supplier rule, and request-offer negotiations, there was something called an INR, or initial negotiating right that attached to that particular tariff cut forever after. How would you do this if a formula were being applied, and nobody was responsible for bargaining for a particular tariff cut? At the end of the Kennedy Round it was decided that if the INR holder would be deemed to be the principal supplier at the time that a tariff got renegotiated.

Norwood: I think Amy's questions point out one of the concerns I have had in reviewing the Kennedy Round. The scope of the round was broader and perhaps the details more intricate than we appreciate at times. Along with tariff negotiations, and efforts to achieve a grains agreement in agriculture, we had a lot of other things going on. Some things came into the negotiations and emerged differently than we expected, and there were other items that came into the negotiations and then disappeared. Any evaluation of the negotiations, I think, should take account of those. Some items we dealt with during the period, we weren't sure whether they were part of the Kennedy Round or not. One such example involves the revised tariff schedule negotiations; we had seventeen of those—and we concluded them by about 1965. The rest were wrapped up in the negotiations. There was also some discussion of commodity agreements, and we had border taxes.

Governor Herter was concerned about the complexity of the negotiations. He did not want to take on more than he had to, and one technique we used with the border-tax issue was to push it off into the OECD [Organization for Economic Cooperation and Development]. Then toward the end of the round, we wanted to make sure it came back, so we didn't lose it. Wyndham White had said the U.S. would be "crazy"—that is the term he used—if we let that issue escape. So, we pulled it back with some resistance from the people promoting it in the OECD.

Fair labor standards was one of the first things that was done on an interagency basis in the Trade Staff Committee. We had two concerns. One, consideration of what should be done when we had evidence of unfair labor standards, and second, the development for the long run of fair labor standards. Herb Blackman and I visited with the ILO [International Labor Organization] director general on that, and we moved that along until we got some adverse comment from our own people in the OECD. That came to nothing in the negotiations. Surprisingly, we had notified George Meany, head of the AFL-CIO and didn't even receive an acknowledgment.

The "chicken war" has been mentioned. We had to review escape clause cases. The most important of those involved watches, but there were others concerning lead and zinc, and even minor things like cotton typewriter cloth. You should have seen all the congressional correspondence we had on typewriter ribbon cloth!

Another matter that came up during this period was the U.S.-Canada auto parts agreement. Some of the people here were intimately involved with that. That was complex. It was handled outside the Kennedy Round negotiations, even though it could have been in that area.

Let me turn briefly to specific points that Amy Porges raised. On NTBs [nontariff barriers] there was some discussion of that. But we had a tradition in the GATT—the U.S. government did—of dealing with NTBs outside the trade negotiations. We had obtained from other countries, and we accorded ourselves to them, a rule that said there would be no quantitative restrictions, no quotas. That was basically the rule; there were a lot of exceptions in the GATT. We insisted that countries observe that rule and we did not have to pay compensation for it. We felt that when the negotiations for trade agreements were first concluded, that compensation was paid for—whatever that was worth—and we weren't to pay again by negotiating downward quantitative restrictions which countries were imposing generally unlawfully under the GATT. So that we didn't have a specific negotiation on NTBs, but we dealt with them in other contexts. ASP might have been considered an NTB negotiation, because that dealt with valuation systems if tariffs were involved.

Amy also referred to the common external tariff, when the tariff increases. We were dealing with that in the linear negotiations, the reduction of disparities was directed toward controlling the increase in the CXT [common external tariff]. There was an argument that on the whole the CXT was higher than the individual country tariffs of the EC were before then. But whatever that argument meant, we were dealing with it both by our desire to have a linear negotiation and by the European Community's desire to have a special rule on disparities.

Then there was the formula tariff cutting. Some have said the linear rule came up earlier. The linear rule came up in 1942 in the Anglo-American financial agreement, as I recall. There were discussions between the U.S. and other governments as to how you would go about effecting a linear reduction of tariffs in light of that obligation between the U.S. and the U.K. then. It had its parallels with agreements negotiated with other countries for the lowering of tariffs overall. There was a French plan at one time in the GATT. There were some other plans before we got to the linear rule in the Kennedy Round.

Regarding floating INRs, we did spend some time at the very end of the negotiations making sure we would not lose that rule allowing countries to lay claim to the loss of benefits where they had initially negotiated the concessions in earlier negotiations. It was felt that the linear rule and this consolidation of obligations which occurred as a result of the Kennedy Round would lose those rights for us, as for other countries. I believe there is discussion of that issue in a four-volume set of analysis done at the end of the Kennedy Round.[8] I am sorry I cannot be more specific. It certainly wasn't forgotten. It does have a history, but not one that would attract those who have written about the round.

Eckes: I have asked Ambassadors Roth and Blumenthal to offer some personal reflections on the Kennedy Round. Let's begin with William Roth, the special trade representative during the final phase of the Kennedy Round negotiations.

Roth: As I mentioned this morning, I came to STR without knowing terribly much about trade and was instructed by all of you. In the thirty years since the end of the Kennedy Round I haven't . . . [focused on] trade, nor do I remember what I once was taught. So in a way I am an innocent, and therefore can look back at the negotiations with a certain amount of objectivity.

I do want to mention one important element in the final period of the negotiation—and that was the close coordination required between Geneva, where the negotiators were, and Washington, where the powers were who had to agree on any final changes in offers and on the final statement. To make this coordination work, Francis Bator set up a distinguished committee, representing State, the White House, Agriculture, Commerce, etc., that could meet at a moment's notice and was in constant communication with us in Geneva. So we were able to move very fast and very flexibly.

I really want to thank the organizers of this conference for sending us some material related to this activity. Not only did it refresh my memories of what happened. But, it throws me into fits of laughter. First, I didn't know that I wrote so well. I am going to read, briefly, some important communications between myself and Mr. Bator and the president, and from them to me. These are all very secretive. They are classified LIMDIS POTATOES. A memo from Francis Bator from William Roth, confidential, LIMDIS POTATOES, subject: canned hams: "Despite the U.S. Department of Agriculture's position, Roth argues that canned hams should remain part of the U.S. offer." April 25, telegram to William Roth from Francis Bator, confidential, LIMDIS POTATOES: "Bator advises Roth to show Jean Rey the U.S. list informally but to postpone actual tabling . . ." I want to get back to the canned hams. Memo for the vice president from Francis Bator, confidential, LIMDIS POTATOES, subject: your meeting on canned hams in the Kennedy Round, 10 A.M., May 6, 1967: "Meeting to be attended by Secretary of Agriculture Freeman, Undersecretary of State Katzenbach, Anthony Solomon, John Rehm, and Edward Hamilton." May 5, letter to the president from Francis Bator transmitting a package containing the pros and cons on the U.S. offer on canned hams in the Kennedy Round: "A) Roth-Blumenthal position for keeping U.S. canned hams offer open; B) USDA position arguing against U.S. canned ham offer, submitted by John Schnittker; C) Secretary of State Rusk's memo supporting Roth regarding binding with no cut as compromise and concession to Secretary Freeman; D) Secretary of Agriculture Freeman's memo for the president, foreseeing serious political repercussions if canned hams offer remains; E) telegram from William Roth for Francis Bator and Secretary Freeman presenting both sides of the case; F) memo for Francis Bator from John Rehm in Roth's office, summarizing importance of canned hams offer to the Kennedy Round negotiations and minimizing congressional and domestic producers' concern over it; G) memo from Assistant Secretary of State Solomon in support of canned ham offer." May 8, telegram from William Roth to Francis Bator, LIMDIS-POTATOES: "Roth needs decision on canned hams by 1500 Washington time." May 8, note from Francis Bator confirming president's approval of compromise on canned hams: "Bind, but not cut."[9]

Well, Mike [Blumenthal], that reflects the ridiculous frenzy of those last days. You read it now and it seems like a lot of boys playing war games. Except in trade negotiations you don't lose lives, you just damage your livers. In the end we did reach a conclusion. Looking back at it, sometimes I ask myself, How useful an exercise was it? Was it successful? Was it valuable?

It obviously was in many ways. Some of the policy and political aspects underlying the Kennedy Round, including the development of the European Community, and our relationships with Europe and Japan, had profound implications. Looking back, how did we do in terms of the bargain we got? In agriculture, I guess we all realized that we wouldn't do very much, because the domestic policies of the various countries concerned wouldn't allow it. And so some of that was smoke.

I do want to mention one episode. At the very end of the Kennedy Round, we were in an impasse. Jean Rey called me at the hotel at night, and said, Can you come over? I called Mike and we came. Jean Rey gave us the last piece of this puzzle we needed to close the negotiations. We called Eric Wyndham White and had a meeting of all the participants at his house. Everyone agreed and the Kennedy Round was put to bed. Leaving that night, I said to Mike, I am not sure that the Japanese ambassador agreed to food aid with everyone else. I don't think you were certain either. So we said we had better go see him in the morning.

So the next morning Mike and I trudged over to the Japanese embassy to see Mr. Miyazawa, the minister, who later became the prime minister. He was a tough little guy. We were told Mr. Miyazawa had broken his leg and couldn't see us. Over the next couple of days, we tried to see him, but his leg wasn't in shape. The next thing we heard was what he said when he arrived in Tokyo. There was a news conference at the airport and he said, Japan never agreed on food aid. I bring this up because one of the areas that I feel we were too lenient, and didn't bargain enough, was with the Japanese. In the long run it probably wouldn't have made that much difference, but I never felt that we held our position, because of policy reasons, as strongly as Bob McNeill [Commerce Department] would have liked. But overall, I think the Kennedy Round turned out pretty well.

Blumenthal: Perhaps I shall begin with a similar anecdote, having to do with canned hams. I don't recall why that particular item was very important at the end of the Kennedy Round. No doubt there was some important political reason at the time why that was a particularly critical product. I suspect in each negotiation there are such products which don't in isolation make any sense but in some broader political sense do make a lot of sense, because they become the key, the last little item, the last little *t* to cross and *i* to dot before the parties to an agreement can sign off on it.

I recall that this was very important in the famous chicken war, where I was the field commander, and the general staff was at home sending me instructions. Chickens didn't seem like a critical issue to the foreign policy of the United States or to U.S.-European relations, but we did have those two Arkansas legislators who played such a key role, so chickens became vitally important. One telegram went out from the State Department asking our ambassadors in the various European capitals and member countries of the European Community to go in personally and see the foreign minister and make representations on some vital matter relating not just to poultry but to chicken parts, known as backs and necks. And so our most senior ambassadors in the various European capitals made their way into the foreign offices to see the foreign ministers and to express the vital interests of the United States in the backs and necks issue. Freddy Reinhardt, our ambassador to Italy, sent back a famous telegram in which he said:

"In accordance with Reftel, called on Foreign Minister So-and-so at 10 A.M. this morning. Emphasized to him in strongest terms vital U.S. interest in backs and necks, urging him to bring to attention of representatives in Brussels this matter. Comment: Foreign minister listened with interest, which is itself a victory, since foreign minister well known to be more interested in legs and breasts than backs and necks." The issue was not trivial, because chicken parts were a critical item at that point to get some larger issue accomplished.

Looking back on the Kennedy Round negotiations, on which we spent four long years, we were in a way pioneers. This was a very different kind of negotiation. In political terms it was very important, because it occurred during the depths of the Cold War. The U.S.-European relationship, the strengthening of Europe, the frontier in the Cold War, was of great importance to the United States. Therefore to conduct a difficult trade negotiation on a new basis in those days, to do it successfully, to do it without causing too much damage in political terms, to maintain the cohesion of our negotiating partners in Europe, which was very important to us, and still get some trade benefits, was, I think, a political accomplishment in the broadest terms.

The keys were Polish hams, and items of this kind. When you put it altogether, I think the Kennedy Round was a substantial accomplishment. We must remember that it happened at a time when economic issues were not understood, except by a few people. Economic issues were not understood to be that critical politically. In the State Department in those days, if you were an economic officer, the chances of making it to the top as one of our ambassadors were poor. You were known as an economic specialist who didn't know much about politics. This of course is foolish, but it was a long tradition. It was widely believed. In those days my good friend Henry Kissinger would openly say that economic matters are for the quartermaster general. He dealt with higher, and more important, issues of grand strategy and realpolitik. Today he wouldn't say that anymore. Henry subsequently has told me many times that he regrets being so ignorant on the vital connection between economics and politics.

So things have changed. Looking back on the Kennedy Round after thirty years, I sometimes wonder whether we haven't gone too far in the other direction. Today we seem to think every political issue is an economic issue. Perhaps truth and justice, as in many matters, lies somewhere in the middle. That leads me to what I think today is one of our most important foreign policy issues and will be, I think, for many years to come—the relationship between the United States and China. That relationship constantly becomes entangled in various economic matters, not that it shouldn't to some extent. It becomes so entangled with them that we lose sight in my view of what are very fundamental, very important political issues, that have very little to do with economics. Such as, for example, the nuclear problem in North Korea, or the Taiwan issue, or our relationship with Japan. These matters don't have anything directly to do with economics, yet everything gets tied up and we get tied up because of concerns relating to some particular economic issue. We always have to remember that there is a close relationship between economics and politics but that they have to be kept in some proper proportion.

I think we were successful, as we said this morning, because we were very fortunate. We were fortunate because it was relatively simple. I suspect that if the present head of USTR were here, she would say, "You people had it easy. You dealt of course with agriculture, but you dealt primarily with tariffs. You did a little with nontariff barriers, for there were still borders in the world. There was no electronic communication. The computer age was in its infancy. It was a very different world than it is today."

I think that she would point out how much more complex are issues having to do with intellectual property rights and pirating. Quite frankly, one of the advantages that I had in Geneva as the head of the delegation is that in Washington the number of people who really understood what we were doing in the delegation was quite limited. That was very helpful. Because you didn't have too many people second-guessing you. There were a few very knowledgeable people that we depended on. I came back to Washington on consultation frequently, and I knew exactly who I had to see. I knew who had what position and how we had to get together. In balance, it was a pretty good team; everyone defended his interest. Today, there are infinitely more people involved. The information explosion has made matters more complex. I think that the number of issues that must be covered is much more complex. So, first of all, the Kennedy Round was a relatively simple thing, although we thought we had a relatively complex set of issues before us. Secondly, I think that today we have a whole new set of problems that didn't exist. Bear in mind that the countries . . . that had a big-C [Communist] designation were out of the negotiations. They floated around some in Geneva, but they really had nothing to do with the negotiations. They were not members of the GATT. Today, there is the whole complex issue of how to bring these countries into the world trading community. That, I am sure, makes these issues much more complex than those we had.

One of the lessons I learned, and I was a relatively young man in those days, is that people and organizations matter. People matter a great deal. Historians debate whether it really matters who is doing what, whether in the great sweep of events, things would happen even if there hadn't been Bill Roth, Mike Blumenthal, John Rehm, John Schnittker, and all of these other people. If they hadn't been there, there would have been a bunch of others.

Would the outcome of the Kennedy Round have been exactly the same? If Governor Herter hadn't been the first Special Trade Representative, if George Ball hadn't been there, or Wyndham White? I don't think so. I think I learned from that negotiating experience, myself excepted, that we were fortunate enough to have the right people at the right place. They were well chosen. Some of it was accident, some of it was choice. That's why I think that it is terribly important that future administrations pay careful attention to those whom they appoint to these jobs.

This has not always been the case. I have been out of the trade business for thirty years. I was back in it marginally during my days in the Treasury. I would have to go to National Security Council meetings and make those final decisions on minor items—they weren't Polish hams, or canned hams, but similar things—to get the Tokyo Round finished. I remember while sitting and listening to Bob Strauss and others explain things, saying to myself, It is the same thing all over again. It is more than a decade later, but it is exactly the same thing.

We have had periods when STR has not been well staffed, when it was not blessed with good leadership. We have had periods when people were thrown into those jobs who were really not well qualified for them, and where for quite a period of time the U.S. interest suffered because they had to learn their job. Some of them were better able to learn it, some were quicker studies than others. Some of them were more successful in attracting good people to work with them than others. So it seems to me that people matter. If this trade business is important, and it is even more important than it was then, then I think it is very important that any new presidential administration understand how vital that job is.

Finally, I think we learned that organization matters. The kind of organization we had worked pretty well. There was a lot of argument, a lot of fights, people made end runs, but that is normal in a bureaucracy. Fundamentally it worked pretty well. That too has not always been the case, as I have watched this process over a number of years. I think we were fortunate in that we hit upon an organizational structure in STR; we had some good people in the different departments. When all was said and done they worked pretty well together. That is a lesson that needs to be learned.

Finally, Joe Greenwald mentioned to me another issue during the luncheon break. It is the numbers game problem. In the public debate over NAFTA [North American Free Trade Agreement] case we got ourselves into the kind of situation where employment effects became a critical issue. People argue whether NAFTA is working, in terms of whether it gains us or loses us more jobs. Some say this is not a good thing and you can't win it. That may be so. I think it is worth talking about.

We had a numbers game in the Kennedy Round, and indeed this occurs whenever there is a negotiation of this kind. Since you can prove anything you want with numbers, I know that we proved decisively and definitely that we had total reciprocity at the end of the Kennedy Round with numbers. I suppose other people who would not wish us well could have proved the opposite. The numbers and measures used are sufficiently imprecise. We had Mr. Preeg here with his 360 [IBM computer], the only delegation that had a computer, and I would say to him, "Prove that we have reciprocity." Ernie would go to work and he would prove that we had reciprocity. If I had said to him, "Ernie, you damn well better prove we don't have reciprocity," I guess being intellectually totally honest he could have done that too. [laughter]

So, I am not entirely sure whether the employment effect is really any different, whether this difference as to whether it creates jobs on a net basis is any more difficult to prove or disprove than was reciprocity in the Kennedy Round. You have to have some kind of numbers to justify what is being done, but you also must have on our end the fundamental conviction, which we had in the Kennedy Round, which fortunately the U.S. as a matter of policy has retained until the present time, that opening up the world and bringing in as many countries as possible into a reasonably fair but open trading environment is of benefit to everybody. And that it has not only economic benefits in terms of raising living standards for people and a more efficient use of world resources, but it also has political benefits because it gives countries a stake in peace rather than in making trouble. You have to have that basic conviction. You have to remember that while canned hams or backs and necks may be critical, they are not really that important. Europe flourished and that was important. The fact that our chickens could no longer be exported to Europe was tough for Arkansas but it didn't change the course of history. But, if the Common Market had broken apart, it would have changed the course of history. And so we must always remember the connection between the economic and the political. We must use the numbers in the end, not dishonestly, when we feel in our heart that we have a balance [to] get this thing closed out, and go on to the next stage in trade negotiations.

Eckes: Ambassador Jeff Lang, the deputy U.S. trade representative, will offer a contemporary comment. Jeff is a former employee of the International Trade Commission, having gained some of his legal experience here. He also served in the State Department. He may have learned even more about trade as a staff aide to Chairman Russell Long of the Senate Finance Committee.

Jeffrey Lang: Thank you, Al. I am probably the only person in the room over the age of thirty-five or forty who owes everyone in this room a debt. It would be wonderful if I could call all of you on a daily basis and find out what grenade I am about to step on, or what cliff I am about drive off of. As many differences as there are apparently in what we do today and in what you were doing thirty years ago, the similarities are striking for me.

Regarding the similarities, the business of hams and chickens isn't any different today. Not less than a year ago I was negotiating an agreement with the Russians on chicken legs, known as Bush legs, because the Russians were persuaded to accept imports of them during the Bush administration. And they rapidly replaced the Russian birds, which I am told were known as blue birds, because of the quality of their manufacture, I found myself briefing the vice president of the United States about chickens roughly thirty years after your efforts. Details don't change in trade. Trade negotiations thrive on attention to detail. One of the things that runs through my experience at the ITC and on the Finance Committee and elsewhere, including USTR today, is that you must have people who are prepared to master detail or you cannot be persuasive with your negotiating partners.

I think the same is true about coordination in complex negotiations, where you have many more players. People absolutely do matter. USTR is gigantic in comparison to the agency you knew during the Kennedy Round. There are now 153 full-time positions at USTR. We have had a flat $20 million budget for the last five years—and lose two and a half people per year to inflation in the federal budget. We are now dealing with $2.25 trillion in trade, so I think in that situation people and coordination matter even more. We had seventy countries sign up on the telecommunication services negotiations in February. It wasn't easy to get the seventy, and it wasn't easy to manage the seventy once we got there. It required an enormous amount of coordination with posts around the world. Some of the great ambassadors we have in the Foreign Service today were essential to us—people like Stapleton Roy in Jakarta, Frank Wiesner in Delhi, and Reginald Bartholomew in Rome. All these people were part of a very large system of interagency coordination in all of the negotiations we go into. We run approximately sixty concurrent negotiations today at USTR.

Now, there are some important differences from thirty years ago. One difference I see is that there is much less focus today on protection and more focus on gaining market opportunities. I didn't experience your period directly, but I came into the system a few years later, in 1974. Twenty-five years ago, we spent a lot of time on Section 201 [escape clause], on arcane dumping interpretations, and I realize some time is still spent on dumping issues, but much less proportionately to the time we are now spending on thrashing out how to create opportunities abroad for the American people. I think that is a significant difference. Obviously, the size of the system is much larger, and you talked a moment ago about the number of players.

I think there are two ways of expanding the system today. One is to involve players whose names begin with *C*—and we are working through some thirty accessions now, most involving former Communist-bloc countries like Russia, China, the Ukraine, and Moldova. We also have a number of accessions in the Middle East, which presents a slightly different level of problem.

There are also the problems of former colonies which entered without having their ticket punched. The interesting thing is how far they have fallen behind. Thirty years ago per capita income in Indonesia and many countries in Central Africa or India was the same. Today, Africa and India are way behind. Most of the literature seems to be saying that the problem is not principally access to the markets of the industrialized country markets, although there are certainly problems in that regard. It is primarily that those markets are closed to goods and investments, because of their own import protection. That primarily arises from the fact that so little of their [tariff] schedules are bound, and when they are bound, they are bound at extraordinarily high levels. This January we obtained a finding that India's balance of payments restrictions—which cover 40 percent of their schedule, quantitative restrictions, licenses, all that kind of thing—are not justified under the balance of payments provisions which were in effect in the GATT in 1967-1968. That's a major finding, because here is a country with 900 million people, a bigger middle class than the United States, and it is almost nonexistent as a trading entity. That seems to us not as it should be. If the Indian economy were opened up, and India became a player in the system, we would all be richer as a result.[10]

Another interesting difference is the levels at which we operate today. We have bilateral levels and the multilateral level that the Kennedy Round obviously represents. In addition, we now have a regional level. It is providing us a new kind of leverage in these negotiations. Without APEC [Asia-Pacific Economic Cooperation], I believe we could not have achieved the Information Technology Agreement, which cut tariffs in the sector worth maybe $500 billion a year. . . . Now it was important that we had a president who was prepared to go to APEC and to urge them to undertake responsibility. But without that effort I don't think we could have convinced the European Union [EU] to reduce its duties as much as it did, as quickly as it did, over the last five to six months.

The pressure of access to capital is making countries realize that opening their markets, and more importantly, binding open their markets, is essential. This is the significance of what you all created, the idea of bindings. Countries are willing to do it today in a way that they might not have been willing to do thirty years ago because they realize it is essential to their development.

I think the depth of the issues is significant because it chews up a lot of time, but in another way that I will raise in a minute—getting beyond tariffs into nontariff barriers, then into new issues like intellectual property and services, and now we are moving into issues even more difficult to address—competition policy, labor, environment, investment. These are all issues that are being actively discussed in the system and it means we need to bring more coordination to the process, more expertise into the process, more congressional committees into the process. I was the lead staff person on the Trade Act of 1988. We had 199 conferees on that bill from twenty-three different committees and subcommittees, of the most complex conference in the Congress up to that day. Today it is even more complicated, involving more committees of the Congress, and I suppose that is likely to continue until we exhaust ourselves.

But this brings me to the interesting questions. One matter is the whole issue of fast track. Some of the things you negotiated in the Kennedy Round resulted in the fast-track process, because the Finance Committee rejected the antidumping agreement and the American selling price agreement. I think the fast-track process has been managed reasonably well by administrations since then as a way to give our trading partners the assurance that we will make a onetime only decision about the nontariff deals we entered into. That question is now before the Congress. The president has stated strongly his view that we should go ahead on that. The interesting part of it is the ability of our trading partners to deliver. We now have serious problems, for example, in Europe with the inability of the [European] Commission to get the member states to deliver on commitments made on their behalf. For example, in intellectual property, in agriculture, it is not the commission that does not want to deliver in most cases, although they obviously must actively defend the actions of their member states. We have four or five member states who still have not implemented their TRIPS obligations—intellectual property obligations.

The next interesting question posed by this symposium for the future is whether there should ever be a multilateral round again. The Kennedy Round began in 1964 and ended in 1967. The last round [Uruguay Round] took eight or nine years. We now have an enormously greater amount of treaty text on the table than we had before we started that round, but even assuming an eight- or nine-year delay, the effective date would be to have everybody take everything on the table off the table and put it back in their pockets until they felt we are down to the chicken legs and canned ham and other final stuff in the deal. In a world of eighteen-month product life cycles, to postpone results for eight or nine years is a pretty dangerous thing to do, and yet last week I was at the thirtieth meeting of the Quad [EU, U.S., Japan, Canada] in Toronto and Sir Leon Brittan of the EU proposed that we start thinking about a millennium round. It might interest you, Mr. Blumenthal, that our chargé now in Geneva, a very talented professional named Andy Stoler, leaned over and said to me, "I know the Uruguay Round took a long time, but a millennium!" We are very cautious about proceeding in that way, although we have not ruled it out. I think it is interesting to think about it in today's world against the backdrop of your experiences.

The third question that this reflective symposium brings out, from my perspective, is the question of MFN. I haven't known all of the U.S. trade representatives. I have known a few of them.

Most of them took no more than six months to start questioning the unconditional most favored nation concept as the basis for negotiations, particularly in the services area. It presents very serious problems today because of the fact that it is not used as a vehicle for trading off concessions in different sectors; it is used as a way of gaining access to markets without making any concessions in the area under negotiation. This is the famous free-rider problem. Because we are a country with global interests, perhaps more global than any other country, it has become increasingly difficult—particularly as we turned away from import protection to obtain foreign market opportunities—to justify free riders in countries that are for many purposes industrialized countries, and surely are advanced developing countries. We don't get seventy countries making a telecom agreement without having some of those advanced developing countries involved. As we demonstrated by not being able to undertake a telecom agreement, nine months before the final deal was made. . . . We couldn't get instructions to agree to a deal, because we didn't have the underlying reciprocity that we needed to justify the deal to the Congress of the United States. I think that was the right decision, and I think it pushed the system forward, but it was a difficult decision. I think increasingly we will see people questioning whether the MFN model works, particularly in the services area.

Finally, there is the question of accessions, bringing in countries that didn't make commitments when they came in as former colonies. We now have 123 countries in the system; I would say about sixty have some type of permanent representation in Geneva, the rest pass through fairly frequently. There are probably twelve—if you count the European Union as one—who are present all the time at everything, but we are going to have twenty-five or thirty new countries in the system sometime in the future. I don't know when. Basically, the pace is governed by the countries that are applying and not by the countries considering their applications. I doubt seriously any of those countries can come in any longer on a political basis. They will all have to come in on a basis that makes commercial sense; and, at the same time, you might have noted a hearing that was largely unnoticed by the press—that was a hearing held in the Ways and Means Trade Subcommittee about a bill to change our trade relations with sub-Saharan Africa. Here is an area of the world in which only twelve out of forty-five or forty-eight countries are now members of the WTO. Only one has a substantial portion of its tariff schedule bound (South Africa), and that at some extraordinary rates of duty. They are obviously way behind in every way. They are almost nonexistent as trading powers. Yet I think that Congress and the administration are moving toward a policy of finding some way to coordinate all international economic policies, including those of the international financial institutions, to bring them into the system by improving their level of their obligation to it. That's an interesting area to investigate. How much can we and should we insist upon as in terms of commitment in order for the trading system to move forward?

Let me just say it is a great honor to speak to you. I should listen to you rather than speak to you, and I wish I could. This job always puts the urgent before the important, it seems to me, and I can't stay. But before I leave today I would be remiss if I didn't single out Bill Hart. Many of the people at this table have helped me, but of all the grenades I could have stepped on, Bill probably prevented me from stepping on 50 percent of them. Many times when I was working on the commission, I would walk downstairs, interrupt Bill, and tell him, I am a little puzzled and I am not sure where I am going. Could you tell me what I am doing? Inevitably, he would come up with the right answer. He is really a model of what the civil service should be. As much as all of you have contributed to this country, to me personally, he stands out. Bill, I appreciate your help very much. It is good to be with all of you, and I wish you a successful conference.

Bator: The remarks especially of Bill Roth and Michael Blumenthal stimulate me to add two short postscripts. One concerns the widespread view that President Johnson was too preoccupied with Vietnam, too involved to pay much attention to what was going on, specifically in this instance to the Kennedy Round. I think that assertion is way off base. He was intensely involved in all the strategic choices, and all the tactical choices we made, and particularly with respect to the agricultural industry, the trade-off on American selling price, down to canned hams. He was an active and intense participant in all that. In fact, the organizational arrangement that Bill Roth spoke about during the last couple of months when he went to Geneva—for a while I guess John Rehm remained as the senior STR person in town—the so-called control group, or command group, reflected the president's determination to retain tight control of the final set of trade-offs we made in the negotiations. The Committee on Trade Negotiations had become a totally unwieldy institutional arrangement for that purpose. It was very important to have a small group of senior-level people who would represent the critical departments involved, with the undersecretary of state for political affairs and the assistant secretary, Tony Solomon; John Schnittker from Agriculture; Sandy Trowbridge, the acting secretary of commerce; and John Rehm, sitting as long as he was still in town as the STR member, meeting with the responsible presidential staff officer in the executive office building and engaging in discussion. In the case of John [Rehm, this] put him in the awkward position of on the one hand representing the Agriculture Department's positions strongly to the rest of us—and through us to the president of the United States—and at the same time acting as one of the president's final advisers in concert with the secretary of agriculture on what he would do if he were president of the United States. Playing that double role is not easy. I remember with great affection John's performance in that role. It was a most difficult position. That organizational entity was set up on orders of the president of the United States with explicit presidential direction to me: "I want those people to act as my advisers in helping to guide the negotiations going on in Geneva."

The second proposition is that somehow we gave away the store for the sake of gaining political foreign policy advantages for the U.S. Here the truth is complicated. It is not only true but entirely legitimate that the president of the United States should consider those trade-offs. We elect him to make those kinds of trade-offs and there is no way in tight negotiations with the EC, France, Germany that he wouldn't have had to, and anyone serving in this central staff position would have had to think about the concurrent negotiations on the special drawing rights, international liquidity negotiations, which were going on exactly at the same time during those last two months. The trilateral negotiations with the British and Germans on force levels and offset were also going on at the same time. The final making of decisions with respect to how far we would back away from a commitment for an open nuclear option to Germany in order to make the nonproliferation treaty possible. All that was going on at the same time. It is certainly true. And the way the White House was then organized, all those sets of issues at the staff level came to the same office responsible for staffing the president on the Kennedy Round. So certainly those considerations played a role.

But I think if one simply puts aside those sets of considerations and looks at the American national economic interest in the trade negotiations narrowly, the proposition that somehow there we gave away too much relies too narrowly on a set of criteria for success or failure that are inescapable in the politics of this world. They are not an appropriate standard to apply to the negotiators, who were negotiating hard and trying to take the other countries as close to the edge as possible.

The proposition implicit in those numbers on reciprocity—that exports are good and that imports are bad—is at best a dubious standard, even if one cares about income distribution and adjustment problems and all the consequences associated with changes in technology, changes in taste, and changes in international trading positions that give rise to dislocations of all sorts. Even if you fully care about those things, a narrow mercantilistic reciprocity calculation strikes me as a very weak one. In the end that isn't what the game is about, even if you consider the American economic interest narrowly. I recognize that this last point is controversial, so I will stop here.

Eckes: Mr. McNeill, we haven't exhausted the subject of industry-related issues. Is there anything you would like to add about the Commerce Department perspective?

McNeill: With respect to American business, the Kennedy Round was viewed generally with considerable favor. However, within the business community at that time, as at the present, there were differing views. There was a very clear view if you were an American exporter that you wanted concessions in foreign tariffs. There was a very clear view if you were an American that imported that you wanted reductions in United States tariffs. That probably would account for 4 to 5 percent of the business population and the rest could be any place at all. There were a lot of businesses concerned about competition that might arise in the U.S. market by reason of reductions in U.S. tariffs, and they tended to be opposed, but on the whole the American business community was supportive.

The American business community was not supreme, but in the global economy very close to it. American producers then were dealing with industrial competitors in countries whose economies had been absolutely devastated in the Second World War. And so there were industries, like the American iron and steel industry, a substantial net exporter at that time, supportive of the objectives of negotiations. There were a lot of American companies at that time that were not only exporting for the first time but, through developing foreign markets for exports, were looking at the prospects for investing in productive facilities around the world. American direct investments were flowing out of the country in some very substantial degree and the American business community was terribly concerned in the early 1960s that if the European Common Market were not disturbed by the Kennedy Round negotiations (that is, if there were no negotiations), that Europeans might take care of their own kettle, to the disregard of the external world. And the prospects that American business saw, not only in exporting to Europe and other industrial markets but their prospects for investing in foreign markets, would have been diminished.

To come back to Ambassador Roth's remark about the Japanese negotiations, the Commerce Department at that time was quite concerned with the settlement with Japan. We thought it was one of the least reciprocal settlements among those with industrial countries. There was some considerable dissatisfaction but not to the extent that the department or its then secretary would have wanted to oppose the agreement in any manner. The specific concern we had with the Japanese settlement at that time was that the normative rule for the negotiation was a 50-percent tariff reduction and if you reduced your tariff by 25 percent, instead of 50 percent, then you would be given a 50-percent equivalency, meaning that you met half of the 50-percent test. In the case of Japan, Japan agreed in the course of the negotiations to bind tariff-free treatment on products not produced in Japan at all. And Japan in many cases bound itself not to raise tariffs on those products. We gave them in some cases, I recall, if they bound a tariff that they had to import because there was no Japanese production, we gave them 100-percent equivalency. In other words, if you don't cut a tariff by 50 percent, which is the normative rule, but you agree to bind the tariff to duty-free treatment, we would give them credit for a 50-percent tariff reduction. It was that sort of thing that we were considerably concerned about.

Kelly: Early in the negotiations there were particular product areas—aluminum, pulp and paper, chemicals and steel. At a meeting in Wyndham White's office, the director general said maybe we ought to have sector groups to try to work out the problems in these areas apart from the linear cuts that would apply across the board. I happened to be involved in the nuts and bolts of the steel sector, where we were faced with the problem of the European Economic Community, which was then represented by the European Coal and Steel Community, which had official rates of 14 percent but applied rates of 7 percent, and their offer was to cut 50 percent—from 14 percent to 7 percent—which meant in fact they would not make any cut at all. We were concerned about that. I know there was a lot of pressure from the steel industry, as there always has been in the history of trade negotiations, on Commerce and other agencies. We found the EEC position intolerable, as did the U.K. and some others.

There was a meeting of the trade negotiations committee to do something about steel, because there was a fear that if steel were taken out of the negotiations this might mean that other sectors would be taken out of the negotiations. So this was a rather important meeting. At lunchtime (the meeting was supposed to start at two o'clock) Mike Blumenthal called me into his office and said, "All right, Kelly, what are we going to do this afternoon?" I said, "Well, we're going to keep beating the Community over the head with its nonoffer," and Mike said, "That's no damn good. That will get us nowhere. We are still going to be in the same deadlock as far as steel is concerned. What else can you come up with?"

I said, "Well, in this sector group we have been working on a concordance of steel tariffs among the different countries [a concordance is aligning tariff positions and rates to see what rates are being charged by different countries on the same products] and we thought we might be able to propose target rates at some point—rates that countries might go toward." He said, "That sounds like a good idea." I said, "Well, we have no Washington clearance on that." That didn't bother Mike much [laughter], and then I mentioned that Roy Denman had been in my office that morning. He had his minister from London come over and he wanted to know what we were going to do that afternoon. I said we would continue bashing the [European] Community. He said that's great, he would continue bashing the Community as well. So I told Mike that I just told Roy Denman this, and if we get out there and do something different, Roy Denman won't speak to me for the rest of my life. (Well, in fact, he has, later on.) And the other thing is that we haven't really finished our work. We don't know what targets to propose. He said, "How many have you got?" I said, "We have about five." He said, "That should get us through the afternoon." So that afternoon, we went out and proposed target rates on steel, namely harmonizing steel rates around some targets that the U.S. proposed. Harmonization greatly appealed to the Community, of course. This got them off their position of proposing phony rates and the discussion focused on target rates. The U.S. liked the target rates, because we already had low tariffs, which meant we wouldn't cut very much, particularly when the targets we proposed were near the U.S. level to start with. So, suddenly the steel negotiations turned around with the U.S. and the European Community on the same side proposing these target rates. Now the U.K. had the problem, because the U.K. rates were much higher than either the U.S. or the Community rates. They were a problem, as I understand it, until the end of the negotiations. Finally, the U.K. came in with maybe a 30-percent cut, but the U.S. cut 10 and the Community 12, or something similar. But it is interesting that if Mike hadn't called me into his office at lunchtime, we might still have had that block over there in Geneva on the steel negotiations. Aluminum, chemicals, and paper might have come out of the negotiations.

Blumenthal: But look what has happened to the steel industry of the world over the last thirty years. With all due respect, Bill, to our brilliance, did it make any difference? Not a damn bit. One of the things we need to remember is that many of the things we negotiate about seemed very important at the time to the health and welfare of a particular industry, but really have very little to do because there are basic economic forces that are much, much more important than whether the rate is 6 percent or 7 percent on beans, or what have you. But look what happened.

Kelly: Mike, canned hams seemed very important at the time.

Norwood: Let's return to this basic concept of reciprocity. We continue to talk about balance, imbalance, what we got, what we failed to get, how we measured it. Paul Krugman has an article in the *Journal of Economic Literature* referring to this as mercantilism. If the United States or some other country removed its tariff completely, the United States would be obtaining some benefit according to economic theory. The reason we focus so much on reciprocity was for domestic political reasons. We couldn't go home with a bad bargain.

I would recast a little what Bob McNeill said about bindings. I think we always described them as bindings free against other country's binding free, and tariff cuts against other country's tariff cuts. I wouldn't knock the idea of bindings free since I recall that was the issue of canned hams. It was the binding free of canned hams entering the U.S., and this was a significant political problem, because they were coming largely from the European Community. But the proportion of canned ham imports into the U.S. from the European Community was much less than from Denmark. To Denmark it was tremendously important even though they were the secondary supplier. Anyway, that was a free-binding issue. I think we spent a lot of time measuring tariff benefits in terms of reciprocity, and should recognize that it is largely a domestic political problem.

Schnittker: I wanted to say that despite the limited results for agriculture in the Kennedy Round, it didn't dampen the enthusiasm of the agricultural sector for trade and even for trade negotiations. As I implied this morning, agricultural trade was expanding in any case. The limited result in the Kennedy Round didn't slow that expansion down; of course, this expansion has not been continuous. It had its ups and downs, but I suspect the volume of agricultural trade now is three times or three and a half times the level of agricultural trade at the conclusion of Kennedy Round, and the value is probably five or six times the value then. In each subsequent negotiation—general or bilateral—the agricultural interests have been more interested, and participating more actively. Of course as the countries of the world—the EC as well as the U.S. and Japan—have to some extent come to their senses on domestic agricultural policy, it has been possible to make progress in trade liberalization concurrent with progress in reducing domestic agricultural price supports and subsidies. The latter in fact precedes the former. I think the typical result is that countries realize they are paying too much in subsidies and supporting their prices too high and they begin to take legislative action to alter that. Then in some subsequent trade negotiations they are able to lock it in with a tariff binding or a promise that they will not expand export subsidies. So I would say that the agricultural community, first of all, accepted the limited results with great patience and equanimity. Their expectations had not been as high as the early rhetoric.

Greenwald: My experiences in the Kennedy Round and the Dillon Round convinced me that the numbers racket was a terrible racket. At one point I was negotiating with the European Community, and the Community negotiator offered a binding on oil seeds of zero duty. We were particularly interested in soybeans, of course. So I went to our agricultural advisers in the delegation and they looked at me as if I were crazy and said, "Greenwald, they are never going to produce oil seeds in Europe." I said, They are not asking very much. Why don't we take it anyway. Thirty years later we are ready to go to war with the Community, when they start to raise subsidies or lay on taxes or duties. That convinced me that it is an absolute waste of time to try to determine what the trade impact will be of reductions of trade barriers.

Now Ambassador Blumenthal has tossed off my worries about NAFTA. When you start to go as far as they have in NAFTA of tying a certain amount of exports to a certain number and kinds of jobs, it makes it even more ridiculous. I think it is a real danger politically. Those of you who are still following these subjects may be seeing that one thing that is causing difficulty for the president to gain fast-track negotiating authority is that everyone is equating it with NAFTA. Depending on which side you are on, and which numbers you want to fool around with, NAFTA is a failure or a success.

I think Hal Malmgren said during the break that the administration failed to answer all the numbers. I tried to talk them out of it as an outsider and they said, If the other side puts up numbers, we have to put up numbers.

Preeg: Let me offer two comments. The first is about reciprocity, . . . it was a lot simpler than you make it out to be. Even on NAFTA it was a no-brainer to show that our access must be increased more than Mexico's, because their tariffs were six times ours.

In the Kennedy Round it was a lot simpler. At the end of the day we were talking not about agriculture but about industrial tariffs being cut (50 percent). After the round I wrote a book about the Kennedy Round and measured the tariff cuts in about five different ways with different variations. For the four major players—the EC, Canada, Japan, and the U.S.—everybody came out 36 to 40 percent. It was a relatively narrow range using different averaging techniques. It was a lot closer to 50 percent than we thought, but it was very close to balance. This was not because the day before I was asked to come up with numbers. These numbers were there. There was a tactical advantage for us to have access to the only computer in town; it was a tactical advantage in not always informing others about what we knew about whether we had more or less. But we knew pretty well. The only exception was the separate ASP package in the chemical sector, which was heavily loaded in favor of us. In other words, they held back much more than we did in chemicals, which was an incentive for us to get this thing through Congress. On the numbers, in terms of mercantilist trade, we had much more to gain. It was deliberately done. The Europeans insisted on it to give us a good reason to go to Congress. A subject that we probably won't get into today—were we really going to push the ASP through Congress? I thought from my junior perspective that we meant what we were saying. We should have put it to Congress in the summer of 1967, when there was political momentum in our favor, when it was proclaimed a success and had support for the sectors. For whatever reason, we waited until 1968, a presidential election year, when people had forgotten about the Kennedy Round success, and then it was dead. That is my first comment on reciprocity.

My other comment, which has come up several times this afternoon, is the central importance of strategic thinking about trade policy and how it relates to foreign policy. In the Kennedy Round it was relatively straightforward, it was mainly U.S.-Europe, something about Japan and others. We talked about George Ball's attention to the big concept, but this type of thinking went on through the four years of the round. Most of it was State Department-oriented, in the department, in the field, and also at STR. It occurred in Geneva and in Washington. This was a foreign-policy initiative. President Kennedy said that. This was a number one priority for foreign policy reasons. . . . And what I have to say is that State and STR kept their eye on the big picture. Treasury as usual had its international financial, balance of payments priorities. Commerce and Agriculture represented particular constituencies. What has happened in the thirty years, though, is that there has been a secular decline in the State Department. They are hardly a player in terms of anything more than the political interest of Japan, China, the geographic areas. The same at USTR. There the striking change is the influence of lawyers. The first STR [and his deputies were] a former secretary of state [Christian Herter], a businessman, Bill Roth, [and] an economist-businessman, Mike Blumenthal. Today they are all lawyers—the U.S. trade representative and her top three or four deputies. For John Rehm [a lawyer] in the Kennedy Round we had to go down three or four layers. Now you have to go down three or four layers before you get to the nonlawyers.

. . . the issues are so much bigger today. Jeff Lang said, Do we want multilateral versus regional free trade, or a new round? Well, we don't really know, because we are not thinking about it. It is not just trade but also investment and intellectual property rights, China, all kinds of strategic, political foreign policy. I defy anyone to point to someone in the executive branch who is really what we would call a strategic thinker in trade policy. The last person, about fourth level in USTR, was Geza Feketekuty. He left two years ago. Since then it has been very hard. I see the present as such a different atmosphere. Thirty years ago European unity was the priority in our intellectual mission. You just don't find that anymore.

Harald Malmgren: I have been uncharacteristically quiet. One thing we should not overlook: to buy political support in the United States Congress, we exempted the whole oil sector, as well as chickens. The oil companies then got behind the Kennedy Round because it didn't hurt them. The textile people were strong supporters of everything we were doing, because they were excluded. They helped to fight the steel people and anybody else who had problems. So in a sense we carved out politically certain sectors—and then we moved on to negotiate where we could.

Issues like canned hams and American selling price—almost all of these politically sensitive issues turned out to be ephemeral. As technology changed the market; the market forces changed and new players came. In the grains arrangement we spent a huge amount of time getting minimum prices on the expectation that world prices would stay above that minimum for at least three years and this was in the presidential documentation, and the minimum price floor was there to prevent anyone from unloading surpluses suddenly and disturbing the world market. Just a year or two later a new administration came in and the minimum prices were completely wiped out because there was a surplus around and everybody wanted to go in the other direction. The U.S. traders wanted to push prices down as fast as they could to crowd out everybody else and to bust the European subsidies.

All of these items proved ephemeral. You really can't anticipate what market circumstances will be. As Jeff Lang pointed out, the product shelf life is increasingly short. Thinking back, what were we doing? We did get to antidumping, ASP. We did have an antidumping agreement. We thought it was covered by the legal framework we worked under. The Finance Committee thought it wasn't and it was aborted. Nonetheless, it started our thinking process. After the Kennedy Round we had a November ministerial in 1967, which Bill Roth attended. There we started the so-called inventory of nontariff distortions to trade. We talked about the border tax issue, and in January 1968 we started a border tax working party in the GATT which went on for a year. All of these things were brought up, but they were not ripe at the moment. They provided the basis for the Tokyo Round and the Uruguay Round.

I recently read the memoirs of Cordell Hull. Two volumes, heavy stuff. Hull was a remarkable man. He laid out, not just in 1934, but actually in 1909, in 1914, the idea that for the United States, which had global interests, the political and the economic and the trade issues were all intertwined and that the U.S. needed to draw other countries in. Most of these other countries did not have the same interests. Only the U.S. had global interests. Therefore, he thought up this reciprocal trade program as a political device to get negotiating and then he pushed almost every version from 1934 onwards personally. During World War II he set in motion a good deal of the postwar planning which developed later. He focused on product tariffs. We had a series of agreements, with the Kennedy Round having the big tariff cut. We began to see these nontariff issues because tariffs got lower. Businesses began complaining about regulatory problems, about overlapping national sovereignty issues, so we began what I call phase 3, a gradual shift from products to the framework of doing business. And more and more we have been talking about this internationally. The negotiations with particular countries are focused on how do you do business in a particular framework. Jeff Lang and I have talked about this, and I guess what we see coming is phase 4, which is discussion not about products or sectors, but about global infrastructure of doing business. What are the rules for doing business, regardless of the product or the service? Then you come to these general questions, such as in the telecom agreement, which is a breakthrough in the conduct of business in the information area, and transcends almost everything.

But there are also country-specific issues. How do you draw China into the system? One of the problems is that Chinese decision making is disaggregated. Everybody is involved in decision making in China—the military, the provincial authorities. There is nobody to commit China. So how do you deal with a China that you need in the system but which can't implement its agreements? That is an infrastructure issue of another kind. We have the regional infrastructure issues. These are the new issues.

Focusing on products and how many jobs are generated from a particular concession is not only a waste of time but you fall into the trap that anybody can prove anything with numbers. Usually, nobody believes the executive branch, so you believe an industry group that has a set of numbers. It is a dangerous thing to get into the numbers game. Basically, the authority of the government ought to be to argue why it is good for America to be in a multilateral system, why we have global interests and have to pursue them, and others don't necessarily have these. We need to draw them in, kicking and screaming if necessary. That kind of argument is not being made at the highest level anymore. There is no Cordell Hull or any of the people here arguing this basic idea of strategy: What is it we are trying to do in the world given that our business interests are global? I think we have learned from the Kennedy Round. It was a part of a gradual transition from an old system to a new system of negotiations.

Eckes: When I think about how the history of the twentieth century may be written, I speculate that the individuals in this room may be remembered for having transformed international relations. In a sense you consummated a revolution far more enduring and significant than the efforts of individual revolutionaries like Fidel Castro or Vladimir Lenin. Your efforts may be seen as contributing importantly to the demise of national economies and the nation-state system and to the development of the open global economy.

Steve Dryden: I would like to ask about the role of Congress. It is one of the most important players. I went back to look at some of the material relating to ASP. There was one memo from the STR to the president in 1967 that said although Congress may not approve the ASP package, it is important to negotiate one. In the end the Finance Committee did reject the ASP package with much vehemence. Russell Long was very, very bitter and adamant about this question when it came up in relation to the antidumping code in 1968–1969.

I want to ask the participants here about the legacy of that episode, because it is a point that people who study trade policy often debate. Is Congress sincere in its protestations about trade policy—the way it is made, the way domestic interests are protected or unprotected? In this case, did the Senate Finance Committee, and Chairman Russell Long, know what was going on and accepted it, or didn't know and then had reason to be outraged later? How did the participants at this table who dealt with the Finance Committee see this issue and its legacy? As you know, the aftermath was a much closer congressional oversight into trade, indeed almost micromanaging.

Roth: The answer should be divided into two parts: What was the relationship of Congress to the negotiations, and to the ASP and dumping agreements at the close. John Rehm should speak because he bore the brunt. As you know, under the 1962 act the Trade Representative's office was set up with an advisory committee composed of senators and members of the House, and I found on the whole this was an effective device. We had Representative Tom Curtis and others involved, and this bipartisan support was helpful. Mike [Blumenthal] sometimes bore the burden, from other senators who came to Geneva and wanted to be entertained. On the whole it was a productive relationship. As was said earlier, [Chairman] Wilbur Mills was the key. He was the most important figure by far. This relationship continued to be critical right through the negotiations. Then at the end, when we divided the ASP into a separate package, which was the only way it could be put together to complete the round, the Fearsome

Foursome—really quite dreadful people—took over. John, I think you ought to comment on that whole period.

Eckes: Who were the Fearsome Foursome?

Roth: Long on dumping, [Abraham] Ribicoff on ASP. . . .

Rehm: Let me take the dumping code first. I hope I am being reasonably objective now. I would say Long's victory was a type of Pyrrhic victory. As I think I said this morning, we made a calculated decision not to exercise the authority given the president in the broadest fashion. There is this telling clause that has endured throughout all the trade agreements legislation regarding the right of the president to modify a duty or other import restriction. In my mind the phrase "other import restriction" could have embraced ASP, as a means of valuation, or indeed could have included the Antidumping Act of 1921 as formulated into an international agreement. Whether the lawyers were right or not, the political decision was made that we probably could not afford to be that bold. And I must say that I was persuaded that the foundation had not been laid for such an aggressive invocation of those critical words, so with respect to antidumping, once interest began to emerge in the Kennedy Round—and I must say I don't know the answer to Amy's question as to where the impetus originally came from—but as things moved it became clear that the U.S. and the European Community in particular were prepared to negotiate a common code, an elaboration of the very skimpy provisions in the GATT concerning dumping. We on our side, the U.S. side, decided, largely for political reasons, as I have said, to stay within the bounds of the existing statute and to work out an international code which would have all of our procedures in it and some of the substantive principles, but without making any clear alteration in the elements and principles of our domestic legislation. That was the basis on which we took the agreement to Congress, arguing that it was a valid executive agreement because it was within the terms of the existing statute.

That's what led to the famous, or infamous, debate that I had with Russell Long one long morning on the Hill. I must say Long played it very skillfully. It finally came down to the question: "Mr. Rehm, perhaps there is no overt change in our law, but aren't you narrowing the discretion of the Tariff Commission in its injury determinations under the dumping statute?" I had to admit that yes, there well might be some narrowing of discretion by virtue of the manner in which the international code was written. This was at a formal hearing before the Senate Finance Committee in the summer of 1968.

Parenthetically, when the president was good enough to nominate me as deputy special trade representative, that led Long, [Everett] Dirksen, [George] Smathers, and [Vance] Hartke—I will never forget those names—to the Senate floor. They said, "Mr. Rehm is an evil man, he is a mischief maker, he is determined to create difficulties between the legislative and executive branches." Needless to say, that was the end of my nomination.

But the point I want to make about the dumping code is: Because we lost Hale Boggs's vote in conference (I still don't know why we did because [Wilbur] Mills, bless his heart, was with us all the way), the conference committee decided to enact this provision which read in effect that the international antidumping code will be valid only to the extent of its consistency with U.S. law. Well, to the best of my knowledge, between that time and the negotiation of the new, more elaborate international antidumping code in the Tokyo Round, that code, with U.S. participation, remained a live document. Indeed, it did guide the manner in which other countries would administer and enforce their dumping statutes.

So, I think Hal's [Malmgren] point is well taken: That the antidumping code, in spite of the difficulties created by the Senate Finance Committee, became the first of the NTB codes that were later subjected to the fast-track authority. That leads me to a final comment on ASP. ASP demonstrated that to take an agreement back to the Congress with no procedural or substantive limitations, none of the protection afforded by the fast-track authority—where it is one vote up or down and that is it—to take a trade agreement back to the Congress, particularly after the conclusion of the negotiating round, poses too many difficulties. It really doesn't work very well. You either have a prior delegation of authority, which the president then exercises without ever having touched base with the Congress again—that was the classic mode—or you really cannot create a proper or appropriate delegation of authority to cover all of the myriad issues of an NTB agreement ahead of time. The ASP agreement, therefore, in my mind stands for the last of the efforts, and unsuccessful efforts, to take an agreement back to the Congress subject to all amendments. It was a failure. On the other hand the international antidumping code is the beginning of a new way of dealing with agreements in the nontariff barrier field.

Eckes: Tom Zeiler, do you have any questions?

Zeiler: I do. I think everyone who has commented today has talked about a greater significance for the Kennedy Round than canned hams and chicken necks, and things like that. I would like any of the panelists to respond to what is a very bold statement on my part. I would like to talk of the impact of the Kennedy Round on diplomacy as it was going on then and afterward. Was there one? We could make a case, for example, that the Atlantic partnership, this Grand Design idea failed, never came to fruition. I was surprised that we heard very little mention of Charles de Gaulle. Certainly whatever negotiations that went on in the Kennedy Round did not keep de Gaulle as a friendly ally of ours. Of course he left NATO in 1966. Finally, the impact of the Kennedy Round on the entire GATT system itself. Could any of the panelists answer whether it has a positive impact on diplomacy, or on the system itself?

Eckes: Let's separate the questions and address the one about de Gaulle. Maybe we also ought to deal with the question of British entrance into the EEC, since that seems to have been contemporaneous.

Norwood: Before I came into STR I spent almost five years at the U.S. Mission to the European Communities; I arrived there the day the commissioners took their oaths of office. I had a keen interest in watching the development of the Community as negotiations went on. Our Mission in Brussels at that time was reluctant to see the EEC forced into negotiations. I spoke to that matter when the Dillon Round came around, because it was thought we would be pushing the Community too quickly before it was ready to deal with negotiations. But, the Dillon Round went on. When the Kennedy Round started, we had before us the revised tariff schedule negotiations. I hesitate to mention that because it seemed so boring to people. When you talk about diplomacy, you point to the significance of that negotiation. It wasn't the tariff adjustments that we had to make. We converted our tariffs in 1930 language to TSUS [Tariff Schedules of the United States] and therefore we had to renegotiate the concessions. To me the significance of that negotiation was the impact on the Community as an entity. The negotiation had started between the U.S. and the EEC in Geneva. The head of the European Community (six countries, but really four since Benelux was acting as a unit) was in the hands of a senior German customs type—Mr. Pingle. He was in demand in the Community for a number of things. He kept getting calls from Brussels to do this and that, and from the Geneva delegation to work on other matters, and the negotiation was getting nowhere. So we decided to pull it back to Washington and we had the people here. It was the first time the Community negotiated as an entity, and they had to decide how to handle those things. They finally agreed that the commission would represent the Community and would be the negotiating vehicle. But, the member states (sensitive that the commission not go too far) each had a representative. Some were from home governments, some from their Washington representatives. So we had a room in State, a conference room, where we had the commission negotiating as a unit. That experience did succeed. It gave them a lot of practice. Whether it was beneficial to us in terms of the Kennedy Round negotiating—strengthening their negotiating capacity—I won't say. But it certainly had an impact on the Community's external relations. I find that quite important. I would also point out, when we talk about the impact of the negotiations, we seem to overlook the contribution that negotiations made on the world as a whole. There has been a tremendous lowering of tariffs. Whether it was in balance between the U.S. and Japan, one can question. Certainly one of the contributions of all those governments working together at that time was to bring about a substantial liberalization of trade worldwide. That was certainly important to us and to our relations with other countries.

Bator: You have to think about the context. One thinks about alliance relationships—the Atlantic Community. As long as the Paris position was governed by General de Gaulle, the possibility of significant, structural architectural progress was going to be blocked. In East-West relations the notion of rapid progress toward the reunification of Germany was the central geopolitical issue of the Cold War and a peace settlement obviously was not in the cards. In that context the foreign policy problem faced by the United States consisted of how to do effective problem solving in various subdomains of our relationship in a way that would not cause a major overload of the politics of any of the major participants. On that presumption that it was a continuing type of thing. And in particular to single out those areas where no progress with problem solving could result in serious backsliding. Trade was such an issue. It was perfectly clear that there was a need for movement forward and for success on that score without creating a major blow-up that would result in a protectionist backlash. It was entirely successful. . . . on the international monetary system, [there was] a large U.S. structural balance of payments deficit and an adjustable parity system that was becoming less and less workable because of international capital movements. In this situation, where movement toward flexible exchange rates simply was not in the cards yet, it made sense to move on with special drawing rights. In our tactical and strategic handling [we sought] to make certain that the blocking intention, or blackballing intention, of Paris would not be realized because they would be isolated. . . . In East-West relations, [we sought] to move Germany from a narrow Cold War Hallstein doctrine, isolating East Germany and waiting for unification, toward something like Ostpolitik, with a kind of early detente. A lot of progress was made. If you take all those things in the context of the incremental-problem-solving view of foreign policy, then the success of each of these acted in such a way as to reinforce and strengthen . . . the American hand. . . . In that respect, without the Kennedy Round of movement on trade, progress on all those other things would [have been] much more difficult.

Zeiler: Would you agree that President Kennedy oversold the Kennedy Round? Kennedy making the grand play for an Atlantic partnership when in reality that was not going to be possible, and even Kennedy knew that by the time de Gaulle had vetoed British membership in the EC? You discussed all of these incremental steps in problem solving. That seemed a little different from the way President Kennedy packaged the Kennedy Round, or the Trade Expansion Act.

Roth: It's a little difficult in politics to talk about overselling by presidents. And I think it is really beside the point, unless expectations have been raised to such a point they are not met and then something happens that is unfortunate. I don't think that happened in this instance. I think Kennedy and Johnson later gave it all they had.

Bator: The test of success on the economic side is protecting and incrementally improving the trading system and the rules of the game which would prevent a sliding back into a jungle, a kind of economic warfare. On the Grand Design, I think in 1961-1962 there was some rhetoric and push in the direction of something architectural that proved infeasible. But I thought by and large that the Kennedy administration and the Johnson administration were very skillful in moving away from that and to practical problem solving on a lot of fronts.

Another example was de Gaulle's disengagement from NATO. That posed an extraordinarily difficult and sensitive political, military, and economic set of issues. President Johnson's performance on that went counter to his leading advisers—the secretary of state, the undersecretary of state, Dean Acheson, and John McCloy, who with justice felt enormous anger at President de Gaulle and what he was doing. The president [Johnson] directed the government management and handling of that, so that very little crockery was broken, NATO came to be reorganized, we managed to hold off Mansfield Resolution pressures, which at that time, with a large pullback of American forces, would have created havoc in German politics. The British army on the Rhine would have pulled back. There is a historian at Vanderbilt now who is looking at LBJ's European policy, both alliance politics and East-West, and is coming to the conclusion, looking at the record, that the performance is remarkable, especially in the context of Vietnam and that the president was principally and personally responsible. I don't regard any of that as being a bad story. I think it is a remarkably good story.

Greenwald: I won't speak as a representative of the State Department. From the years of 1958 to 1963 I was in the American Embassy in London, and I will give you a slightly different perspective from Bernie Norwood's view in Brussels. The British and the EFTA countries were all in favor of reducing tariff barriers and the common external tariff. I am not sure what Grand Design you were talking about, for it was not evident to me in the American Embassy in London. We supported the European Community, when the British set up the EFTA, along with the Scandinavians and a few other countries. You heard the story from Francis Bator, what happened when George Ball went over and changed U.S. policy because he didn't like us at sixes and sevens. When he was asked what we wanted the British to do, the answer was, Join the Common Market. When that failed in 1963 with de Gaulle's veto, the next best thing was to have a major tariff negotiation, which the Kennedy Round provided.

James Lewis: I would just like to add one thing. I was glad that Hal Malmgren referred to Cordell Hull and his beginning of the whole process. I also think there were others in the State Department, like Henry Grady and Harry Hawkins, who continued that. That whole process resulted in the State Department becoming the Wicked Witch of the West, because it had to fight the other agencies many times in those thirty years before the Kennedy Round. They had a great struggle, and they made great progress. Progress in reducing trade barriers was not made only in the Kennedy Round but in all those years from 1934 to 1962. The Trade Expansion Act wasn't the first time Congress authorized 50-percent tariff reduction authority. The first 50-percent tariff-cutting authority was in the [Reciprocal Trade Agreements] Act of 1934. I think that should be remembered, and the fact that the Trade Agreements Committee had to yield to the Trade Staff Committee in STR was understandable. But I think we [in the State Department] should also get the credit for a lot of good work before then.

Eckes: Mr. Blackman, organized labor became critical of trade policy after the Kennedy Round. Why?

Blackman: I might comment about labor participation. During the Kennedy Round I was not aware of any great labor movement pressure except in the textile area. This was handled separately with the Long-Term Cotton Textile Arrangement. The Tokyo Round was different because you had the proliferation of the advisory committee structure. The Labor Advisory Committee was quite active—troublesome if you will—in terms of the negotiations. By that time the labor movement as a whole had become attracted to restrictions in the Burke-Hartke bill, so they were reluctant participants at best.

If I might make another comment about the issue of jobs and trade that we hear about all the time. The numbers are always produced; indeed, I think I produced some numbers; and the Labor Department produced some numbers. I don't think any of them are really accurate or relevant. On the export side it is perhaps a little easier to make calculations. On the import side, we don't know where the imports are coming from, where the content is, so the numbers are largely imaginary in my judgment.

McNeill: Mine is a personal comment, Mr. Chairman. I want to thank you, Bill Hart, and your colleagues responsible for putting on this conference. This has been a wonderful opportunity for me to revisit several very important and happy years in my life. It is true, as others have said, that this was a remarkable group of people. We worked together intimately over a period of several years. History brought the right man to the right job at the right time when Bill Roth took over leadership of the negotiations. He was a wonderful leader, he inspired all of us, he made each of us, whether deserved or not, feel important. He listened to our views, he accommodated them to the extent possible, and I want to thank him for his personal contribution to what I consider a mightily important endeavor and a very successful one.

Hedges: While we are making tributes to participants, I would like to mention another individual. His presence here is certainly due some recognition. I refer [to] Francis Bator. Francis at that time was relatively early in what has become a distinguished career. He was the principal assistant to McGeorge Bundy, and the two of them were the conduit of Governor Herter to the president. They very effectively and successfully maintained all the liaison and provided the decisions which STR needed at particular critical points. Governor Herter, and other members of the staff, were in regular, if not daily contact, with Francis Bator. When you consider that Francis was always available whenever he was needed, and he frequently attended our conferences and meetings, and bear in mind he was the principal assistant to the guy [McGeorge Bundy] who was essentially the chief of staff to President Johnson and their responsibilities covered the universe. This was the period of the Vietnam War and various other things that occupied policy.

I could illustrate by an anecdote the role that Bator and McGeorge Bundy played. It was at least two years into Governor Herter's tenure as special assistant under Johnson. I was in his office one day and he was expressing frustration and the need for some guidance and support and he said, I would really like to talk to the president about this. I said, Why don't you call him. He looked at me in surprise as though it was a totally new idea. I left. Two or three hours later I ran into him again and he was like a little boy with his first bicycle. He said, "Irwin, after you were in here I called the president and was connected immediately and I am going to see him within the hour." Well, I think that is a good illustration of the important role that Francis Bator and McGeorge Bundy played in keeping the lines clear between STR and the president.

Rehm: My favorite anecdote relating to the Kennedy Round came at a cabinet-level meeting to evaluate the negotiations, with President Johnson present to review where we stood and whether we should finally accept the deal or not. I can recall several of the cabinet secretaries going on at some length about the political problems that this will create if we accept the deal, much congressional criticism, difficulties, etc. President Johnson said, using words I do not need to relate literally, but in essence he was saying, "Well, I get that sort of thing every day. What I want to know is," and I was so impressed with this, "is whether it will be in the national interest to conclude the Kennedy Round and accept the deal or not? That's what I want you to tell me, looking ahead fifty years." I sat there thinking, That's what a president of the United States should do.

Bator: I am reminded of the difference between the way the White House foreign policy staff was operated then and is organized now. There was a handful of us. Bundy was special assistant for national security affairs. He encouraged us to deal with the president and have our own relationships with the president. All of us had an enormous portfolio. I had all of U.S.-Europe, and foreign economic policy, with two assistants—one named Lawrence Eagleburger and the other one Edward Hamilton. The point is: It made the White House foreign policy staff reach out laterally to the departments, to the key people, to work with the people on trade, instead of the enormous big central bureaucracy of its own that gets in the way between the rest of the government—the secretaries, assistant secretaries—and the president of the United States. I wish the whole White House foreign policy establishment would shrink back to the size of the basement of the West Wing.

Norwood: We need to add a comment on the Tariff Commission and its role in those negotiations. During the Kennedy Round the commission acted as a service organization and did an enormous amount of work but never did take a policy position. When the Kennedy Round began it was charged with doing a factual analysis and providing us with digests of all U.S. imports that could be considered for negotiation. It also provided confidential advice, in the sense of an evaluation of what the effect would be of tariff concessions, and that set of information was kept by me locked up in a safe. . . . I took the relative pages to each one of the TPSC [Trade Policy Staff Committee] meetings and had it available for anybody who wanted to ask. I do think we should all bear in mind the very substantial work that the commission did during that period. It was relied on by all of us as objective and professionally sound, factual information and evaluation. . . . Bill Hart remembers all that work, and was responsible for a great deal of it. He came along to succeed someone else from the Tariff Commission who had a shorter, but very useful, life. That was Tony Kenkel, who retired after "only" forty-two years of government service.

The Tariff Commission played a unique role in the trade agreements, interagency trade agreement process. Originally, the Tariff Commission was a full member of the Committee on

Trade Agreements. When peril points were enacted by Congress, the commission decided it could no longer have anything to do with a policy role and gave up its voting rights. So it participated in the trade agreements committee as a nonvoting member, but it provided a lot of good, objective material.

Roth: I want to pick up on something that John Rehm said. President Johnson himself, this amazing man, when one of these critical issues had to be decided, including an important element in the Kennedy negotiations, would have his cabinet in and he would have outside people too. On one occasion I remember Clark Clifford being there. Then he would go around the room asking for comment. When that was done he would make his decision. What other president did this? None that I am aware. Kennedy didn't do this.

Eckes: Thank you, Ambassador Roth, that must conclude today's discussion. I want to thank all of you for your participation and the excellent commentary. Thirty years after the event, the Kennedy Round remains vivid in your memories. The record of our discussion today will add perspective and understanding to that very significant episode in American trade history.

✧ CHAPTER FOUR

Reviewing the Tokyo Round

Participants: Lawrence Fox (Department of Commerce), John D. Greenwald (STR), William T. Hart (ITC), Dale Hathaway (Department of Agriculture), Gary Hufbauer (Department of Treasury), Jules Katz (Department of State), William B. Kelly (STR), Alonzo McDonald (STR), Amy Porges (STR), Howard Samuel (Department of Labor), Robert S. Strauss (STR), S. Bruce Wilson (STR), Alan William Wolff (STR). The ITC Historical Society, in cooperation with the Jimmy Carter Presidential Library, held this roundtable session October 5, 1998. The moderator was Alfred E. Eckes.

Alfred Eckes: The Tokyo Round of multilateral trade negotiations produced some of the most significant accomplishments of President Jimmy Carter's administration. The round, the seventh held under the General Agreement on Tariffs and Trade, began twenty-five years ago, in September 1973, with a ministerial in Tokyo, Japan. It concluded in the spring of 1979. While multilateral negotiations concentrated on reducing industrial tariffs, the Tokyo Round was the first to address, on a broad scale, nontariff barriers. The results included a number of codes pertaining to government procurement, subsidies and dumping, product standards, customs valuation, and import licensing.

This session begins appropriately with the reflections of Ambassador Robert Strauss, who was President Carter's first special trade representative, and the cabinet-level executive most involved with concluding the Tokyo Round of multilateral trade negotiations. Ambassador Strauss must leave early to meet other commitments, and after he concludes we will move to a round-table discussion of the Tokyo Round with other participants.

Robert Strauss: While I like to think I had a significant role to play in the Tokyo Round, my colleagues mastered the subject and I think I mastered the politics of how you start and move a set of negotiations. So I played to my strengths; and we used their strengths to get the substantive work done. I am not saying that in all modesty, because I have many faults, but modesty is not one of them!

Let me set the stage for how I came into this job and sought to reactivate the negotiations. I had concluded that I was not going into the Carter administration. I had been chairman of the Democratic Party for four years and I wanted to return to private life. In March 1977 President Carter called and asked if I would be interested in the STR [Special Trade Representative] job. He had heard that I would be interested, and the truth of the matter is that I had some interest.

A distinguished columnist, Joe Kraft, had been talking to me about Carter's election. He suggested that I try for the STR job. It didn't have bureaucracy, and you could get something done. He said that if we didn't do something about our trade policy the world would go to hell in a handbasket.

So, when President Carter called I had some general familiarity with the need but limited familiarity with the subject. I went to his office and we spoke for a while and I told him that I would think about it and let him know. Around seven o'clock that night I received a call from Senators [Russell] Long [D-La.] and [Abraham] Ribicoff [D-Conn.], who were having dinner in Senator Ribicoff's apartment. They had consumed a good deal of wine by the time they called me, and they were a good deal jollier than I was when I answered the phone. They were each on a phone extension. Senator Ribicoff said, "We understand that you turned President Carter down on taking the STR job."

I said, "That's a damn lie. I didn't turn him down. I told him I would think about it."

"Well," he said, "we gathered you weren't very enthusiastic."

I said, "'We gathered' wrong. I said I would think about it."

Russell then interrupted and in his Louisiana Southern drawl, which I hardly recognized, said, "Bob, wouldn't you like to be a hero?"

I said, "Russell, I would love to be a hero. I never had that role before."

He said, "Well, I'll tell you what we are going to do. Me and Abe, if you take that job, are going to make a hero out of you because we are going to get you everything you need."

I said, "Is that right?"

He said, "Yeah, and so it will be clear to you, if you don't take the job, we are going to run you out of town."

I went into see the president the next day and I said, "I talked with Russell Long and Abe Ribicoff, and I'm prepared to take that job. They explained the job a hell of a lot better than you did."

So that launched it. And the first thing I did was to ask a few people to recommend a deputy. Of course their answers all ran to Alan Wolff. Half a dozen other names bobbled up—various people, people in industry—but everyone came back to the fact that when I realized what terrible shortcomings I had for this job—I lacked skill and experience—I needed Alan Wolff. I invited him to join me for lunch at the Madison Hotel, and he explained that he would be very interested in going to Geneva to handle that job.

I said to him, "Alan, I would love for you to be my deputy, but not in Geneva." Well, he was only interested if he could go to Geneva. He liked veal and he liked foreign travel. . . . He didn't mention work, but he did mention all the things he liked about the European side of it. I said, "Alan, that is the one place you will go only for a day or two at a time. I need somebody that understands this subject. We will get someone else for the Geneva job."

He was a bit unhappy, and not in very nice humor, when we broke up that day, but I did have a commitment from him that if I needed him, he would take one of the two jobs. He hoped . . . it would be the European one, which of course it was not.

We then had the domestic deputy nailed down, and next Alan and I began to look around to see who could handle the

Geneva job, and we looked at a lot of different people. As I recall, it took several months before we located Al McDonald, and I talked the damn fool into coming into my office. . . . He didn't want to come in. He was head of an important consulting company and making about three or four times what he would make in government. I convinced him that it was a rare opportunity for him to do something with his life that he would never have another chance to do. He had been in the private sector long enough. One thing led to another, and after two or three visits, McDonald and I shook hands and we had that part nailed down.

During the course of that search Alan [Wolff], Bill Kelly, Geza Feketekuty and others were briefing me on one subject after another. I really had very limited knowledge, but it was obvious that this [Tokyo] round was dead in the water. No one had an interest in it. The Europeans didn't want to be touched. The Japanese, as usual, were taking no initiative and were sitting on their hands. There was no enthusiasm in this country of any kind whatsoever for moving on these negotiations. I don't believe there was 5 percent interest on the [Capitol] Hill for the round.

Jimmy Carter, however, believed that there was nothing more important than to revitalize and get those negotiations started. Despite the fact that they were dead in the water and despite the fact that I had just completed four years as chairman of the Democratic Party, following the tremendous McGovern defeat, this was not a very appetizing time to take on this new job. But we got off and running.

One of the early things Alan and I did—I think it was within sixty days of the time I came into the position—was to meet in Brussels with Willy [Wilhelm] Haferkamp [vice president of the European Community], who was in charge of the European Commission's external relations. Alan and I went over. As I recall, this was before Al McDonald came on board. We two—and Geza Feketekuty—went over to talk to them. They were about as negative as we had anticipated, and we were really making little or no progress. Wolff had briefed me on the fact the one thing they feared more than anything else was that we would try to destroy and eliminate the Common Agricultural Policy (CAP). So in the middle of the discussion, I said, having discussed it in some considerable detail with my colleagues, "I'll tell you fellows something that you ought to understand. The United States has absolutely no intention of destroying and eliminating the CAP." That stunned them. They were really shocked, because they feared the United States intended to use negotiations in agriculture to destroy the CAP.

Haferkamp said, "What do you mean by that?"

"I mean that we want to get our nose a little further under the tent, and we are darn sure going to insist on some liberalization [in agriculture], but we have no intention of destroying it [the CAP] or eliminating it."

You could see the relief in their faces, and they looked at each other. After about ten minutes they took a recess for about an hour. I will never forget it. They came back and the whole tone of the discussion changed, and all of a sudden for the first time, in my judgment, we had something of a dialogue going between the European Community and ourselves about the Tokyo Round, and it proceeded from there.

Haferkamp, I think, had Finn Gundelach with him at that time. He handled agriculture for the EC. Gundelach . . . was an important player and one we could not overlook.

As we moved along, Bill Kelly was on the staff. Dick Rivers joined us from the Senate staff. Bruce Wilson came along. We put together a pretty good staff, particularly for a fellow who wanted to play the role I had to play. . . . It is almost embarrassing to say this in front of a group of professionals, but the truth of the matter is I never really had time to learn the subject to the extent I should have. I had good people around me and I could go into a meeting and always could make a noise like a trade negotiator, but I surely wasn't. When it came to substance, I was weak and I knew it. But I had strengths and my colleagues would play to my strengths where I had them and I to their strengths where they had them. My strengths were of course in the public arena—in moving this negotiation with Japan and Europe, and in handling the American Congress.

I don't think that it is an exaggeration to say that we met with 535 people on the Hill—we met with almost every single congressman and senator—most of them several times. We broke them up. Wolff and McDonald would come over and they would take on a few. Others would. Jules Katz, who tried to teach me something but he didn't teach me too much, handled some more.

I haven't thought about the Tokyo Round in close to twenty years. We had good help on the Hill—Barber Conable [R-N.Y.] and Bill Frenzel [R-Minn.] were a tremendous help to us on the Republican side of the House and Charles Vanek [D-Ohio] worked hard with us on the Democratic side, as did others on that committee. In the Senate, Ribicoff and Long did what they said they would do. They stayed with us and tried to help us—and did the best they could. Bob Dole was helpful when we could get our hands on him, and I was trying to get my hands on him most of the time. We moved forward.

We made a determination early in the game—and I kept saying to Wolff and McDonald—we have to make this bigger and bigger and bigger, [adding] more and more to the table. It has to be so big that no one can stand the failure. I don't think the Europeans or the Japanese realized what we were doing as we kept loading that table. We loaded it up and went into areas not [negotiated] before. When it came time to pass what we had drafted, again we played into an area where I had strengths.

I remember two breakfasts I hosted for Washington lobbyists—about fifteen or eighteen Democrats and an equal number of Republicans. We had thirty or forty lobbyists over to the White House mess for breakfast. We went over what we were trying to do and asked each to be responsible for helping with a certain congressman to get their industries and clients involved. We made assignments. We assigned each of those lobbyists three to eight different members of Congress that they would be responsible for, and we followed up on it. They reported to us just as they did to their home offices. They were all pleased to be there. Most of them were not eating breakfast in the White House mess every day. The Republicans, who were out of office, were particularly pleased to be there.

We went before the House Republican Conference [to discuss the Tokyo Round agreements]. I remember that John Rhodes said to me, "You are walking into a hostile group here but we will handle them." When we got through, he said, "Strauss, I'll tell you one thing, go back and tell those friends of yours on the Democratic side that we will give you a higher percentage of votes than they gave you." And, as a matter of fact, he did.

Well, we judged the Tokyo Round agreement to be a good work product. I don't think any of us gave it A+. I think all of us gave it B+ or maybe an A–. There were things we left out. I am amazed as I look back, for example, that we left out services. I don't remember why. We just had so much to do that we couldn't get around to everything. Whatever it was, we put together a working team. We made the office of the Special Trade Representative a center office in Washington. When people came to town, they came to our office, something unheard of. Our trade negotiations were at the center of what was going on and indeed turned out to be one of the real accomplishments of the Carter administration. President Carter promised me he would give his full support and never back off. He certainly lived up to his word.

Finally, I want to tell you a story about how the press observed passage of the Trade Agreements Act of 1979. In the *New York Times* it occupied the important right-hand column of the front page. The same thing for the *Chicago Tribune*, the same thing for the *Los Angeles Times* and other great newspapers. The *Washington Post* reporter, for some reason, failed to show up and the *Post* had not one line.

When I got up the next morning [after Congress passed the act] I could not wait to read the marvelous story about what a wonderful STR we had in Robert S. Strauss. I could have cared less about the staff. [laughter] There was not a damn line in there. I almost had a stroke.

About two or three hours after that disappointment, a messenger brought something from the White House, a copy of a note President Carter had written to Ben Bradlee, then editor of the *Washington Post*. He said, "Dear Mr. Bradlee: When they passed the Kennedy Round, your paper carried it as a front-page story, praised it to the sky, but when Bob Strauss in this administration passed the Trade Act of 1979, it didn't merit one line in your paper. You ought to be ashamed of yourself." Signed, Jimmy Carter.

About six months ago Ben Bradlee called me and said, "Strauss, I'll buy you lunch. I have something I want to show you." He brought with him a photostatic copy of that letter. He said a collector had just offered him $3,000 for that letter, and he said, "I turned it down, but I did bring you a copy."

Let me add one other thing. We had simply first-rate people, and the country owes them a great debt of gratitude. Nobody ever had more loyal and more dedicated partners in a venture than I had with Alan Wolff and Al McDonald. I don't mention their names, and not the others, to denigrate what others did. But not to mention them would certainly be a shame.

Eckes: At this point I would like to turn to a general discussion with our distinguished panelists. At the beginning it is important to understand why the Carter administration made a decision in early 1977 to continue the Tokyo Round process. Ambassador Strauss told us that the Tokyo Round was dead in the water when the Carter administration took office. There seems to have been no enthusiasm in Washington or Brussels or Tokyo. Why did the administration choose to continue this process? How did the executive branch agencies see the situation in 1977?

Jules Katz: I did not view the negotiations as dead in the water. They certainly were not moving very rapidly and there are a number of reasons for that. I am not sure I can remember all of them, but basically it was a problem of moving other countries along—primarily Europe, which is the other major participant in any of these negotiations. With a presidential election in 1976, our own government was somewhat in disarray and that certainly slowed the pace of negotiations. In the end the negotiations lasted five years. This was the amount of time provided in the U.S. legislation [Trade Act of 1974]. It has been my experience, through the Uruguay Round, that GATT rounds conformed to a Parkinsonian rule—namely, they expanded to fill the amount of time made available by the U.S. Congress. In 1976 we were two years into the negotiations, so I didn't consider the round dead in the water. It certainly wasn't moving very rapidly and needed a burst of enthusiasm and new leadership. That's what the new Carter team provided.

Eckes: What was the perspective from the Agriculture Department, Secretary Hathaway? As I understand it, the Ford administration had pressed negotiations on the European Common Agricultural Policy, and, as Ambassador Strauss pointed out, one of the first things the Carter administration did was to assign less emphasis to attacking the CAP.

Dale Hathaway: Yes, that is correct. Coming in with the new administration in 1977, I can say that agriculture, and particularly the bureaucracy that controlled trade policy in agriculture—namely, the Foreign Agricultural Service—were dragging their feet. Unless the objective of the negotiation was to destroy the CAP, they saw no purpose in it. They were totally focused on that, and they had rejected European interest in some type of commodity agreement. The enthusiasm for the latter was very low in USDA, a view I shared.

There was no significant enthusiasm for the Tokyo Round. American agriculture in general did not have the export orientation that developed in the late 1970s and continued in the 1980s and 1990s. So the USDA was not one of the pushers until we made some changes in policy and some changes in personnel.

Eckes: Ambassador Strauss suggested that there was not a broad constituency in Washington—outside government agencies—in favor of the Tokyo Round. Do others on our panel recall which outside groups were most supportive?

Lawrence Fox: There was enthusiasm for the Tokyo Round in many departments of the government and especially in the Department of Commerce. I was deputy assistant secretary for international economic policy and had responsibility for Team A. Team A was the part of Commerce that was trying to liberalize trade. Team B was concerned about the textile agreement, the steel agreement, major automobiles, and they were always dragging their feet. Although these team designations are allegorical, it was the responsibility of the secretary of commerce to settle these internal disputes. Very few disputes got to him. He ran the textile negotiations and the steel negotiations personally, because there was a large congressional and political aspect.

The rest of it was all details. I was in charge of the details on the trade liberalization side, and the enthusiasm in the Commerce Department was evident to me from major companies and the State Department. The State Department had a foreign relations objective. The State Department always has a foreign relations objective. My job was to figure out how to work with the State Department, sometimes with Agriculture, always with Treasury. These were the power brokers within the executive branch, and there was generally a coalition available, if you knew where to look for it. I didn't have any doubt that the trade negotiation would end on the last day of the congressional authorization, as Jules Katz has suggested, and end successfully as it did.

Katz: I think there was support for negotiations. I don't know that I would call it enthusiasm. There wasn't the level of emotion attached to trade negotiations in the 1970s, and earlier, compared to what we see currently. A broad coalition of companies, industries, and agriculture—the major farm organizations—were supporters of trade. You have to view the Tokyo Round as continuing the trade liberalization policy initiated decades earlier. It was sustained by government policy and government leadership. To some extent it was mobilized by the executive through such devices as the Williams Commission [U.S. Commission on International Trade and Investment Policy, Albert L. Williams, chairman], appointed in the early 1970s after the Kennedy Round, to make policy recommendations.

There was support for trade liberalization, but the level of public participation was more limited than what we see at the present time. There was support in the business community—the Chamber of Commerce, the Business Round Table. But, some industries were clearly on the other side. Larry Fox mentioned textiles. The problems of the automobile industry came up later. At the time of the Tokyo Round we had lost almost all of the unions except perhaps the dockworkers. Until the Kennedy Round we had support for trade liberalization from the UAW, the communications workers, and transportation unions generally.

Howard Samuel: There was very little interest on the part of the labor movement as a whole in international trade and not a great deal of enthusiasm for the Tokyo Round except at the staff level. There were some staff people at AFL-CIO headquarters on Sixteenth Street who were interested—and they were mostly opposed, as I recall.

There were some individual unions with an interest in trade and therefore had an interest in what was to happen in the Tokyo Round—the steelworkers, the textile and apparel workers, the consumer electronics unions had a particular interest. But the extent of staff knowledge was limited, because few unions considered trade of primary importance. As far as the Department of Labor was concerned, we were committed to doing our best to support the administration, but to do it in such a way, hopefully, that would retain the support, or at least the neutrality, of the labor movement as a whole, because one thing the labor movement had in those days, and still has to a certain extent, was a great deal of influence on Capitol Hill. We saw that during the debate over NAFTA.

Alan Wolff: I think it is important to view the Tokyo Round as part of a continuum. Soon after the Kennedy Round concluded, preparations were under way for what should follow. I remember my first trip to Geneva, as a representative of the Treasury Department. It had a dual purpose—one was to explain the Domestic International Sales Corporation [DISC] as a benefit for mankind [laughter], and the other purpose was to serve on Bill Kelly's delegation for a two-week meeting on the standards code. It was dreadful. It was a difficult, slogging process, but it was the kind of thing that occurred with interagency delegations of seven or ten people advancing U.S. interests. But it was very slow. These negotiations could not have come to a conclusion without political will, and political will was not then present.

The genesis of the Tokyo Round is to be found in the breakdown of the Bretton Woods system. The U.S. imposed a surcharge on imports in August 1971. The Smithsonian agreement, reached on December 18, 1971, provided that there would be bilateral talks on trade. Teams were set up for discussions with

Japan, the European Community, and Canada, among others. I served as a staff attorney for the Canadian talks. Some countries offered some concessions—including the Japanese—but basically they all said that if you want something significant from us there must be a multilateral negotiation, and you will have to give too. That led ultimately, under the leadership of George Shultz, to the Tokyo declaration in September 1973 launching the round.

But other countries would not negotiate without the U.S. having a mandate from Congress. As you remember, there was a change of administration in August 1974. We were busily impeaching the president. The stunning thing is that the Congress of the United States gave absolutely sweeping power in trade negotiations to the executive branch at the time when it was in the process of removing the leader of the executive branch. The 1974 act established the fast-track process.

As to why the Tokyo Round didn't come to a conclusion earlier, it is important to remember that the Ford administration was, from the viewpoint of foreign delegations, a caretaker administration. Moreover, the deadline wasn't close. In a GATT round, people negotiate against a deadline, usually the expiration of U.S. negotiating authority. There were also contentious issues, such as the shape of the table on agriculture.

There were times when I was over there as acting head of the delegation for six months in 1975 that the French refused to talk to me. I didn't realize what a boon that was at the time. It was another French tactic to avoid anything taking place whatsoever. We didn't know what direction to go in. We were talking about a commodity stabilization agreement—the grains accord—versus market liberalization. We had a doctrinaire position to dismantle the CAP, the Common Agricultural Policy, which was a nonstarter, but we had to swear fealty to that objective. My nomination was held up for three days in June of 1977 by Bob Dole until I pledged myself to agriculture. He submitted three pages of questions that got longer answers. Basically, the answers could have been summed up, "Yes, sir."

Regarding the tariff formula, the Europeans very much wanted us to get rid of our tariff peaks. These were part of our landscape—like the national parks—and involved politically sensitive areas. Agricultural exporters were desperate to get started, and wanted the U.S. to take a purist line, as did the Department of Agriculture. You never knew exactly whose side USDA was on, except for Dale Hathaway. There were people under him who worked very hard at assuring that we were never able to show any flexibility in the early days and come up with anything like a response.

One other thing regarding domestic constituencies: The most enjoyable meetings were perhaps with labor folks. They were distinctly opposed to most of what we were doing. It was an honest, clear exchange of views. They were very open about it. Industry presented a mix. Some industries were more sensitive to imports; others wanted to see market access move forward and they were worried about the links to agriculture. The agricultural groups, for whom we were working hardest, I felt were often the most unforgiving. Those were tough meetings, because whatever we were doing, it was wholly inadequate at all times. The talks were comatose, with a lot of work going on in the agencies. But in terms of momentum, until Bob Strauss took over and we took the trip to Brussels in mid-July, 1977, we were stuck on tariffs, couldn't move forward on agriculture, and we did not have the political leadership to break the deadlock.

William Kelly: There were a number of dreadful meetings—not merely on the standards code but also on subsidies and countervailing duties, government procurement, licensing, customs valuation, antidumping. They were all dreadful. But this was part of a number of dreadful events in the whole progression of U.S. commercial policy from 1934 on.

I view the Tokyo Round as a continuation of the trade liberalization process, which started with the 1934 Reciprocal Trade Agreements Act in the Roosevelt administration. This was followed by the GATT, which multilateralized negotiations, then the Kennedy Round, the Tokyo Round, and now the Uruguay Round. Over the past sixty-five years there has been a progression in which we not only eliminated most of the tariff protections in the developed world but got into domestic policies that were once sacrosanct from negotiation.

To sustain this process you had a lot of dedicated people who pushed liberalized trade, not only in the United States but around the world, like religious zealots. I am one of them. A number of people in the State Department, when I worked there, were highly motivated people. They pushed the U.S. government and the public whenever they could towards international trade negotiations, which they believed, quite correctly, were to the advantage of the United States.

Eckes: Perhaps we should turn to a discussion of the actual negotiations. Ambassador McDonald, could you explain the negotiating objectives and how they were pursued?

Alonzo McDonald: To return to something Bob Strauss said earlier, I couldn't figure out why he wanted to speak to me. I was a total outsider, I was an independent, a violent independent, one opposed to both parties. I had just earned enough money to buy a yacht. I told Bob Strauss that if I had to sell a yacht to be in a Democratic administration, I was not a candidate under any circumstances. He assured me that I could keep it. But I never got to use it. For the next eighteen months we really worked around the clock. My view was not a government view at all, and I think that was the reason I was invited in. Many of my contemporaries in government at that time were absolutely appalled at the way I conducted the negotiations. Jules Katz told me this was the strangest set of negotiations he had seen. At the time Jules was there I think he thought I was rude, improper, ran overtime, and did a poor job. My view was that this was a commercial negotiation.

I had a different perspective, because I had not been a part of the government process. I was the head of McKinsey and Company [a management consulting firm] during the mid-1970s, and I had watched the stock market drop 45 percent during the last half of 1973 and 1974. I saw us move into the worst recession since World War II. I had spent ten years in Europe, six years living in Paris watching what was happening on the international scene. I had watched the dwindling of investment, a lack of interest in doing business across borders. I was watching one thing in particular: what were millions of people thinking about in terms of acceptable levels of risk, particularly with entities operating internationally.

It is one thing to talk about what governments do, but the main problem we have in business is that governments serve as barriers for doing business. To the degree we can reduce those barriers, that is a major step forward. All one has to do is to look retrospectively at what happened to the numbers in the ten years after the Tokyo Round concluded to see what the impact was. From a governmental point of view, results linked to policy changes were one thing, but from a private business point of view, which is mine, it was quite another. Our interest was in government attitudes and in progress in reducing trade barriers, leaving the way open for the millions of independent decision makers to trade across borders.

I was a reluctant entry to the negotiations. I only came after I was assured by both Bob Strauss and the president that they truly wanted to do a deal. I did not find anyone who was excited about that, except a few people who were real professionals and were in STR. In my initial discussion with the department, there was a nucleus of people who thought it would work out in due course, but I did not find a lot of enthusiasm. From my perspective, that carried through for most of the negotiations.

At the close of the Tokyo Round I received a series of cables from most of the cabinet secretaries who had been members, or represented on, the Trade Policy Review Group. Almost all said it is probably a good thing that the round has ended. Then, they said, We regret very much that the following was not accomplished. Each seemed more interested in maximizing his or her department's special interests than optimizing an acceptable overall deal for the country. Those were my letters of congratulations! I think that was a fair reflection of the degree of enthusiasm that we had initially.

I had undertaken an unusual commercial negotiation. It was a government negotiation, but it was not like disarmament or a peace treaty, or managing a political alliance. . . . I was really interested in what we could do to improve the assessment of millions of international business decision makers of the level of risk they considered important to do business with each other and to work across borders. That was my focus, and it differed from that of most people.

After I was sworn in, I expected a few days of briefings . . . but Ambassador Strauss said, There is a meeting of the Labor Advisory Group today and Howard Samuel is chairing it. He said that he was supposed to go, but he wanted me to go instead. I went alone and I met Howard. I quickly understood how little support we could expect from organized labor. Howard was most congenial and helpful all the way through. I want to commend the team around this table because we would not have been able to complete successfully the negotiation and gain its approval in Congress without their support. We had a superb team.

From my point of view, we did not consider it a Geneva or Washington team. I commandeered people when we didn't have the experience locally in Geneva, including a young John Greenwald and Dick Rivers, who were willing to take over the customs and countervailing duty code and move it ahead. And Bill Kelly, who didn't even consider tariffs his speciality, but he spent many long nights with me, as he noted, pulling those difficult negotiations through to an acceptable conclusion.

From a commercial point of view, I viewed our efforts as three separate negotiations. The first one was between the departments in Washington, to come up with the instructions. Then second was always these negotiations between Geneva and Washington on the instructions. How can you do them, how can you follow them, how can you move? And then finally you have the negotiations with ninety-nine other countries.

Incidentally, I am not sure it is possible ever to send a negotiable set of instructions to a negotiator. Perhaps it is in times of war and peace, but I am not sure it is feasible in economic negotiations, because I don't know that anybody ever was willing to give enough in instructions to make a deal. So, the negotiators have to stretch and to take risks, but the only way you can take a risk is because you have political support. The thing we had was Ambassador Strauss, who had a direct line to the president. We had authority to deal on a political basis. When I was in trouble and being criticized the most, I would call Bob Strauss and ask, What do you want me to do? He would say, I want you to negotiate. I would tell him that this is the best we can do. He said, It looks like a good deal to me. Move it ahead. It was on that basis that much of what we accomplished was done. Those were the dynamics of the situation I was in as head of the negotiating team in Geneva.

I found the members of the delegation had a lot of competent people—mostly middle level—some of whom turned out to be real stars. There were others who I think were really put out to pasture. But all had allegiances to individual departments back in Washington. There were one or two who were really STR people, but the rest were departmental representatives and had their own private communications back to headquarters. They were all organized from a functional point of view. They were all specialists. No one really had an interest in a final deal. They were only interested in maximizing results in their particular segment of the negotiations. That approach was clearly going to be a loser. Whether we made a deal or not depended on how they were doing in separate functional negotiations.

In about sixty days I reorganized the group, much to their amazement. I said, You will remain functional specialists but I will complete your personal evaluation forms based on a new set of assignments which will be by country. So we split the duties. We set up a series of teams to deal with the big entities like the European Community, Japan, and Canada. For the smaller countries, we assigned three or four to an individual member of the delegation, and I wrote to the heads of other delegations negotiating in Geneva and said, Here will be your predominant representative. This is the person who is concerned about our negotiations with your country.

We set up a central communications unit under Harvey Bale, who had the computer skills to do this. We set up a simple reporting mechanism so we could have a series of continuing discussions going on with as many countries as possible. We wanted a central report on what was going on in those separate discussions.

So the pattern shifted completely as we reorganized and reoriented how the negotiating group worked. My attitude was, you have got to negotiate a complete package with your designated country, not just in the one area of your specialization. You will be responsible whether we come up with a deal with the entity or not. That shook the Geneva group up quite a bit, particularly when I said it doesn't make any difference to me how you want to be judged at the end of the day. Your department in Washington will judge you as they see fit, but my performance reviews will be on the basis of how you negotiate and handle your responsibilities as a full-scale negotiator dealing with countries. I even assigned our public relations person [Bob Meyers] Colombia and Zaire. He was astonished but did a very good job. In fact I took three or four of these people back with me to the private sector later on because they had excelled in very difficult situations.

There was another element. It was important to assess who we were negotiating with. I spent considerable time—almost more time than studying the issues of the Tokyo Round—trying to get information on what had happened during the Kennedy Round, and what happened during the Dillon Round. I firmly believed that the Tokyo Round was just a continuum. From my perspective the object of the game was not to stumble but keep making steps, keep making steps forward. I think that approach fit directly with President Carter and Ambassador Strauss's views. It was clear we had to have a deal with the Europeans or we had nothing at all. We looked to see what was going on. At that point in time my deputy was a superb professional, and the European Community's head of delegation in Geneva was also a superb professional. But they had been negotiating with each other for about three and a half years, and had reached the point of animosity where it was difficult to meet in the same room. Consequently, in the reorganization we did not assign our person to the European team but put him on a different team. I decided that the only way to have a deal was to build a personal relationship with Sir Roy Denman, the EC's lead negotiator resident in Brussels.

What impact did U.K. membership in the EC have on the Tokyo Round? First of all, it gave the EC their principal negotiator. Roy Denman had headed the EFTA team in the Kennedy Round and was a real pro. He understood the need to come up with some type of a next step forward. He and I built a good personal relationship together, and we also avoided going to general GATT meetings unless we were absolutely instructed to do so, because those were always dysfunctional. They followed the pattern that Alan Wolff and Bill Kelly mentioned. The only time we went to the GATT for a formal meeting was when we truly had something to put forward and had the advanced countries at least willing to support it. The EC, represented by Roy Denman, would be with us in those situations.

The French were a problem. I had to give Roy some help there. I had spent six years in France. I had made my living there and I knew a lot of people. So I did things that, again, were strange. I think I am the first U.S. ambassador ever to meet privately with the heads of the French agricultural unions in their own building, and address their questions on a first-come basis. I met with most of the major French business organizations. We knew we could never get the French government's support, but we hoped that we could move them toward neutrality. We were using the same strategy of dialogue that we did with organized labor in the U.S.

I even met informally with a French parliamentary committee. It was of course totally unofficial, but during a reception I dealt with their questions about what was going on. We also spent as much time as we could with some of the French officials, and I even had some private friends, the heads of eight or ten of the largest French companies, who invited the director of external economic relations of the French Ministry of Finance [Bertrand Larrera de Morel] over to a dinner at which I was the guest of honor. He had not met most of them. He was a fine guy but he had strictly governmental, not business views. The French CEOs favored it—they were not afraid of international competition. They knew that was the wave of the future. They were much more afraid of the barriers their own government was putting up to retain the status quo in France.

I mention these items to illustrate how the dynamics of a commercial negotiation differ from the way you conduct a typical governmental negotiation. I know that most of the members of our government, except those in STR and Ambassador Strauss, vigorously disagreed with our approach, but that was the way we conducted the negotiations. We also maintained control over what was going on locally in a way that was excessive by most standards. I am sure almost everyone from Washington disapproved. I drafted a four- or five-page memorandum, and Bob Strauss sent it out to visitors, saying, This is what we expect while you are here. McDonald is in charge of the delegation. We want to know exactly who is meeting with whom and what you are discussing, and what the issues are.

So we employed a lot of tactics in the course of the Tokyo Round negotiation that were different. We also did not operate by regular hours. We frequently went on twelve, fifteen, eighteen-hour sessions. I am sure that annoyed many who thought it was unnecessary. But when we had key decision-making units in from the capitals, we did not let them go home until we had everything we could accomplish within reason. So, we had a lot of late-night sessions. These are not atypical in a company situation or union negotiation but are sometimes atypical in a government situation. They were a standard pattern for us.

I even missed an important occasion in Dijon to meet with the delegation from India one time when the [trade] minister was in from Delhi. I met with the Indians and it was a total waste of time. But it was necessary to do. It had to be checked off on the list, as we exercised whatever courtesy was required. My good wife and I also did a fantastic amount of entertaining. . . . we had all the key people from every delegation in and out. We built a lot of personal relationships. And then we entertained a lot of members of Congress. For them we developed a full presentation, a series of slides acquainting them with what we were doing and what the status was. We held question-and-answer periods and provided fairly elaborate dinners, after which they could meet with leaders of the delegation. As we neared the end of the Tokyo Round, we invited within a six-week period the leaders of all twenty-six of the ISACs—the industrial sector advisory groups. They came in, we had a half-day session set up. Again, this involved a presentation on the overall negotiations and where we stood. Then, we listened to them, with their individual points of view, and tried to respond. This was a standard pattern. I think we neutralized quite a number in opposition initially.

In a few cases we found advocates that we would not otherwise have had. That aspect was set up by the group in Washington.

Strauss had me flying back and forth across the Atlantic about once a month. When I was here in Washington, I usually came for two or three days, spent about two hours at STR, and then the rest of the day would be on Capitol Hill, seeing six or eight people. The next two days would be making speeches, particularly in alien territories. As illustrations, I addressed the rice producers in New Orleans and the agricultural people in California. I spoke to the dairy industry in Minneapolis.

We also tried to neutralize major opponents. We invited over leaders of our two biggest union groups, who initially did not want to come at all. But, Sol Chaikin [of the International Ladies Garment Workers Union] and Murray Finley [of the Amalgamated Clothing and Textile Workers] came with their delegations. I think those were very constructive visits as well.

The Tokyo Round involved an unusual set of circumstances. Fortunately, we had the political will and the leadership at the top from Bob Strauss and President Carter. They said, We are going to do the best deal we could and complete the negotiations. From my business perspective we began to see movement. During the ten years following the Tokyo Round the attitude of independent business decision makers as to what was an acceptable level of risk in international affairs, in cross-country business arrangements, began to blossom. From my point of view, that was the real accomplishment—and that was what we set out to achieve in Geneva with the Tokyo Round.

Wolff: I would like to second what Al McDonald said about instructions from Washington. I was given the role of acting head of the U.S. MTN [multilateral trade negotiations] in February 1975. Hal Malmgren was the deputy STR in Geneva at the time and he was leaving on the next day. He said, "In tomorrow's meeting, accept the EC's proposal on agriculture." It was purely on a question of the shape of the table—about how to approach agriculture in the round and I dutifully went to the meeting and accepted the EC's proposal, which seemed fine to me. Then a cable came in from Washington which seemed to be totally at odds with what I had just done. This upset me since it was my first act in the chair and I asked the EC chief negotiator, Theo Hijzen, to come out of the room and look at this cable I received from Washington. I asked him, "Is there any way on earth that what we agreed to fits with my instructions in your view?"

He said, "No, I can't see how it would." So I went back to the delegation's offices and called Bill Seidman, who was then chief economic adviser to President Ford, and told him what had happened. He said, "Was there a blow up?" I said, "No." He said, "Fine, go ahead. Get on with life." It didn't matter.

I am sure we sent out a lot of instructions to Al McDonald from Washington that had a number of things like that in them.

I would like to add another comment on how we revived the negotiations in mid-July 1977, and also about the role of the Geneva delegation versus the roles that Strauss and I played working from Washington. The negotiations were stuck. They were stuck largely over tariffs and agriculture. Bob Strauss went for his first meeting with the European Commission in the Berlaymont building, which was subsequently closed for asbestos problems. It was a very historic building, with many pictures of the Community's founders around the big table of the commission. Strauss, Geza Feketekuty, and I sat on one side, and there were three primary vice presidents of the commission—Willy Haferkamp, who was the External Relations Vice President; Finn Gundelach, who was in charge of agriculture; and Viscount Davignon, known to us as Stevie, who was in charge of the internal market. Roy Denman was there as director general for external relations in DG-1 [Directorate-General].

When the meeting started, Willy Haferkamp said, Roy Denman has drafted a proposal on tariffs. He handed it across the table to Bob Strauss, who looked at it for about ten seconds and threw it back across the table, saying, "This represents no progress at all." It had a few tariff formulas on it; it was an algebraic-looking document. There was no way on earth Bob Strauss could have recognized what was on that piece of paper. What he knew was the Europeans would not offer anything that was adequate. And he was quite right. It was wholly inadequate.

Then Bob said, "Let's talk about the agenda for the day." They said we would meet from nine to ten on this and from ten to eleven on that. Strauss said, "Where's the press conference?"

They said, "Press conference? We don't know that we will have anything to announce. Why would we want a press conference?"

Strauss said, "At the end of the day I am going to appear before the press and I'll either praise you or denounce you, depending on what we do in this room today." At three o'clock that afternoon, standing before the cameras, with his arm around a perspiring Willy Haferkamp, they announced they had a breakthrough on the tariff formula. They had an agreement in principle on how to move forward.

Roy Denman came over to me and said, "Alan, we will not be dictated to by this Prussian." It was an interesting misidentification of Bob Strauss's roots. The fact is that by the end of the session a partnership began to form—that partnership is the one Al McDonald alluded to with Roy Denman and the shuttle between Brussels and Geneva. We had a partnership with Europe, and the fact is you need a partnership with the European Community to move major trade talks forward. It will not be moved with a partnership with Japan. There is no one else out there to move trade negotiations. It was true in the Uruguay Round, it was true in the Tokyo Round. Mike Blumenthal, I am told, did not have that sort of relationship with Brussels during the Kennedy Round. Rumor has it that he asked for the removal of his counterpart, Theo Hijzen, and in response the European Community made Hijzen a full ambassador, which he had not been before.

At home we were managing a domestic process. We had an advisory committee system established by the 1974 trade act that we thought was going to be a millstone. It had over a thousand advisers arranged on fifty or sixty committees. There were twenty-seven ISACs (industry sector advisory committees); there were nine labor sector and nine agriculture committees. Fortunately, the labor committees decided to meet as one group. There was less proliferation of meetings.

In fact, the ISACs were an enormous strength for two reasons. One is we got an enormous amount of information. We were better informed as negotiators than anybody else around the table and I think Al McDonald would agree. One of the major U.S. barriers that we had enshrined for a long time was "wine gallon, proof gallon," which made the bottling of Scotch whiskey in Hartford and

Philadelphia economically rational.[1] The EC desperately wanted to get rid of that. We understood that the market was headed to so-called white goods [gin, vodka], and the concession was thus not as valuable as the Europeans thought. That was the kind of insight that very few others had. They would negotiate for historic objectives and we would negotiate for what our industry, agriculture, and other advisers were telling us they could live with and wanted.

We involved the Congress in a way that had not been done previously. We gave our cable traffic to the Congress—to selected staff members who were cleared. We had members of Congress going to Geneva very often and—to the absolute shock of both the recipients of this process and the professionals—attending the most sensitive private talks. Bob Strauss would wave to the chiefs of staff from Ways and Means and Finance who were over there and say, Just come into the room and sit quietly on the side. They were, as only Strauss managed to do, captured. They could say what they wanted to say outside of that particular meeting—whether they liked it, didn't like it—and report to their bosses completely on what was going on. The result was that this advisory group in the Congress, the advisory group in the private sector, became part of the process to the extent that they had a stake in the outcome and believed in it.

The Trade Policy Review Group that has been alluded to and the Trade Policy Staff Committee and the Trade Policy Committee—three different levels—were responsible for hammering out policy. For the staff group this meant officials at the office director and deputy assistant secretary levels. For the TPRG and the TPC, officials at the assistant secretary and undersecretary levels were involved. On all issues we managed to come to agreed conclusions.

Al McDonald, of course, captured the people who were drafting instructions and put them right into negotiations. We largely let Al McDonald do what he was doing, I think. I don't know if that was his perception at the time, but Bob Strauss and I would go to G-7 summits and Al would come. There was a political commitment driving the process. We didn't try to do the negotiations from Washington, or to run to foreign capitals. But where we could be of assistance to the team in Geneva, we were.

On one occasion Strauss went up to Ottawa. The Canadians had insisted on sectoral negotiations. The reason they wanted these is that they had a great notion that they would trade access for their raw materials, but no access to their own market for our manufactured products, in return for which we would give them complete access to the U.S. market. It seemed like a very neat deal from their perspective. I won't put on the table here exactly the technique that Strauss used. It is a colorful story. He had a small meeting with the trade minister, Jean Chrétien, who later became prime minister, and in about fifteen minutes Strauss convinced him it was absolutely hopeless to pursue this line. There was no support anywhere, it wouldn't go anyplace, and it was the last time the Canadians raised the subject.

The important thing, I reiterate, was to have a partnership with the Congress and the private sector, and with our primary foreign negotiating partner, the European Community.

McDonald: Let me elaborate on the point involving our instructions. We took our instructions extraordinarily seriously. We studied them, and when they were not confidential we filed them with the GATT. I had a deputy who was well accustomed to all protocols, and so they were all followed. We assessed through the presence of those in Congress and those from other departments and the private sector where we could come out. We did not operate alone. I frequently responded to instructions . . . by saying, "Here's as close as we can come. Unless I get instructions to the contrary, we will proceed along these lines." I never got a counterset of instructions. We were also on the telephone regularly, two or three times a week, so we were not operating in separate units depending only on cable traffic. We really were in personal communication. Whenever it was a tricky situation, Alan and I would be on the phone with Bob Strauss and the three of us would say, "How should we go?" We went forward literally as a team, but they did give me extraordinary latitude to run the operation in Geneva and to manage the tactics of the negotiations in what was a strange manner, I am sure, for most governmental people who observed.

Eckes: Little has been said about negotiations with the Japanese. Were these quite difficult?

Hathaway: One of the little-noticed, and more important, developments in the round was that for the first time the Japanese established some quotas for products that had been absolutely banned from importation. These included beef (later enlarged), orange juice, and some other products. We spent an afternoon and evening in Washington toward the end of the round with the Japanese minister of agriculture, the Japanese ambassador, and their trade negotiator. I have to tell you that I have never seen a more brutal session.

Ambassador Strauss was not kind to the gentlemen from Japan. As we went to dinner at the ambassador's residence, the ambassador said, I have never spent a more difficult, depressing afternoon. The answer was that before the end of the day we had an agreement that there would be a beef quota, there would be an orange juice quota, and some other things. That turned out to be a very significant element in opening the Japanese market for agricultural products. I personally had little to do with it, but I certainly enjoyed watching.

McDonald: Let me comment for a minute on the Japanese situation, for I spent a lot of time on it. They had a minister for external economic affairs named Nobuhiko Ushiba, who understood something about world activities. I spent a lot of time in Tokyo, going back and forth, at the same time I was in the private sector living in Europe. I helped to open an office in Tokyo, and worked with Japanese private clients quite a bit.

Negotiating with the Japanese really involves the Chinese water treatment. It takes a great deal of persistence and patience, but there is almost nothing instantaneous. You have to go in tiny steps. We did. We dragged them along. We spent an awful amount of time with them. We also identified a number of deputies and subordinates who were very good. For example, Hidetoshi Ukawa, the number two person on the Japanese delegation in Geneva. He was absolutely superb. It did not hurt that he was a relative of Minister Ushiba. This was an informal way that we communicated frequently, avoiding some of the formalities that normally followed.

When we did have delegations in from Japan, we carried on long, long negotiations. I can remember on one occasion some of our Washington friends left about 8 P.M. and I think the

Japanese wondered when they were going to get dinner. Instead, we were also trying to get a bourbon quota in, as part of some agricultural exchanges at that point in time, so I brought in bourbon and hors d'oeuvre at about 8:30 and we finally ended our session about 1 A.M. They were leaving to go back to Tokyo the next day. So I said everything had to be done that night and we did it. We came out with a reasonable agreement.

We got everything we could in Geneva from the Japanese. I remember when we did get the orange and beef levels, Bob Strauss was naturally disappointed, as we all were. He said, "Al, you have to go to Tokyo and start this all over again." I said, "Bob, I have gotten everything I can out of that situation. There is no point in going to Tokyo; I have other things to do."

He said, "I'll send Alan Wolff." I said, "Poor Alan gets so many dirty jobs. Spare him this one." He said, "Alan's got to go." I don't think much came out of it. We did not give up on the Japanese. They were not willing participants, but we kept them close, and after we had a deal with the EC we would bring in the Japanese and bring them along. At the Bonn summit meeting, I was in side meetings with the Japanese the whole time. Strauss said, "This is the best time we have, since everyone is here." While they were in the main meeting of the Seven [G-7], he said, You work the Japanese over, because we are either going to have some concessions here at Bonn or I am going to make a speech saying the Japanese are holding up the whole thing. So with that lever, we negotiated on the side all during the Bonn Summit Conference.

Samuel: I think that there is one thing we should not neglect in our review of the negotiations. They were not all on generalized broad-scale global discussions. Much attention was paid to domestic constituencies whose support was necessary to the final result in Congress. To this end the special deals—the side deals—that Ambassador Strauss and Alan worked out with the steel industry and the textile industry not only neutralized those industries and their unions but gained their support in responses which in turn neutralized the AFL-CIO. Probably that is one of the main reasons the bill passed with over four hundred votes in the House of Representatives.

Fox: As I see it, the Tokyo Round was aptly named. It boldly stated that Japan was to be invited and encouraged to play its full role in the international economic scene, and to do so in accordance with the rules of the game. By the last years of the round—after 1978—it was obvious for all to see that Japan preferred to play its lone hand and to accept those aspects of the world trade regime that were either convenient or basically innocuous from Japan's standpoint. For example, tariffs were definitely not a problem; there were other means to deal with excessively competitive imports. . . . so long as licenses were required and customs inspections took place, there were ample means to hold up or stifle imports.

Regarding government procurement, the formalities of any conventional agreement were acceptable so long as Japan could continue to treat its enterprises as inside or outside the definitional fence, or as *de minimis*—e.g., hospitals, university laboratories, etc. Regarding technical standards, [Japan would] rigorously enforce [them]. If necessary goods could be held up virtually indefinitely for inspection and testing. Safety standards in Japan were tailored to Japanese products, and testing had to be performed in licensed Japanese facilities located in Japan.

And the Japanese no longer needed export subsidies. Thus international antisubsidy agreements were acceptable and even useful in combating competition. Of course, really unstoppable subsidies, such as the artificial exchange rate and cheap credit, were built into the system.

Regarding capital and credit, a word of explanation is required. The Ministry of Finance nominally controlled the banks, created credit through the budget deficit, supervised the stock market and foreign lending, and determined or structured the tax system. Interest rates were hardly free to allocate capital or savings.

Each major industrial group had its own superbank. Naturally these banks always had funds for major members of the group. The life's blood of the industrial economy was this financial system that provided capital and credit by making the government's deep pockets readily accessible to major industries through the top-tier banks that were part of each industrial group. And each industrial group had its own export-import trading company to do the international buying and selling. The automobile industry chose *not* to follow this pattern, proving to be the exception that perhaps proves the rule. Subsequently, major electronics firms also broke away from the old pattern.

The scope of this financial relationship became obvious *only* as the result of the current Asian financial crisis. And the cozy system of preferential treatment among firms within the group was unbeatable—either because prices did not determine product selection, special rebates or discounts were possible, or the old-boy network naturally gravitated to known and familiar products. Of course, the so-called Fair Trade Commission did not prevent these arrangements but, in certain instances, facilitated them.

Of course, this all seems a lot clearer to me now than at the beginning of the Tokyo Round [1973-74]. The U.S. government believed somehow, or simply assumed, that Japan would mature into a typical market economy in the fashion of the U.S., Europe, the U.K., and the independent former members of the Commonwealth, such as Canada. Therefore, we evolved no strategy to work with the European Community to bring about this result. Nor did we work with Japan to put pressure on the EC regarding agriculture and industrial policy issues, dispute settlement, and codes of conduct. Perhaps no such grand strategy was feasible in any case. U.S. hegemonic power was a lot easier for columnists and academics to write about than for the U.S. to put to work for our benefit or that of the world economy more generally. The present U.S. economic situation in the global perspective appears to confirm the reasonably satisfactory results derived from reliance on market forces and financial strength.

John Greenwald: In a basic policy sense, the process of organizing the negotiation was essentially thoughtless. By that I mean we were dealing with a continuum. People—all the negotiators as well as political appointees—truly "wanted to do a deal," as Al McDonald said. They accepted the past as prologue and proceeded along those lines without any serious deep-rooted questioning of assumptions. I did, and I think everybody around this table did, the same thing.

Japan was left out. The core problem with the Japanese was not addressed nor was there any effort to address those problems or related problems stemming from central government control over East Asian economic development during the round. We did not set up parameters—What is essential? What would the U.S. insist upon or walk away from? I think the driving force in a negotiation like the Tokyo Round, as in the Uruguay Round, is in the first place a deep-rooted notion that a liberalizing deal of almost any sort will pass whatever minimum objections are required by constituencies back home, and is essential. The fear of failure, more than the exhilaration of success, drives the process. The process ends when U.S. authority runs out, because everybody is more concerned with the implications of failure than they are with a careful analysis of the benefits of success. The issue that puts this in perspective is the way that Japan was treated more or less as the tail of the dog. The focus of the attention was always on Europe first and then with the rest of the world.

Wolff: Our intelligence capability in terms of knowing what the restrictions were in Japan was wholly inadequate then and remains inadequate to this day. We did not understand the structural barriers and did not deal with them effectively. The round was not designed to deal with those barriers. The subsequent round [Uruguay Round] did not deal with those barriers either.

This absence of understanding is evident in the following story. There was a twenty-seven-inch snow fall in February of 1979. I was snowed in over in northern Virginia. A Japanese delegation came into town to negotiate on leather, a very sensitive subject for Japan, because of minority politics. They made me an offer, which I should have accepted, but I foolishly rejected it. They said, "We will allow as much leather to enter Japan as would cover automobile seats coming back to the United States. As long as none of the leather stays in Japan physically, we can accept that." I responded that this was an insult, that this is not the way world trade is conducted: "We can't agree to some sort of deal whereby what we sell to you can't remain in your country."

In retrospect, I was profoundly mistaken. It would have been a phenomenal deal. The second oil crisis hit within a short period of time, and Americans ran out and bought small Japanese cars of increasing value with leather seats. It would have been a magnificent deal. Instead, I pressed the Japanese delegation and got a quota out of them.

There are a thousand similar stories. On beef we got a quota for hotel quality beef, 10,000 metric tons. The Australians were very unhappy because it was high-quality beef, not grass-fed beef. They thought that discriminatory. We would tackle each problem individually. The Japanese of course welshed on the deal, and they purchased a cut of meat that perhaps many around the room would not immediately want. That was inside skirt, a cut not very attractive to the Japanese consumer. The result: we didn't sell a lot of beef at the time.

I think there was real progress in the Tokyo Round on the broad issues the round was designed to deal with—things like the tariffs, which did matter. But did we open the Japanese market? No. Has anyone done it since? No.

Eckes: Secretary Hathaway, I know you wanted to make another comment about agricultural negotiations. Perhaps you could also assess for us the results of the agricultural negotiations.

Hathaway: Unlike some of the other sectors, there were really two negotiations, or perhaps, two and a half in agriculture. One was the tariff and access negotiation, which was largely STR, and the Department of Agriculture played a supporting role. As part of their demands the European Community and others had insisted that we must be involved in grains negotiations. You will remember this came shortly after the great grain robbery and the U.S. embargo of soybeans. We had signed a supply-purchase agreement with the Soviet Union and therefore everybody wanted a grains agreement, particularly those dependent on imports. Because of the complexity and the need to have countries like the Soviet Union involved, those negotiations were moved to UNCTAD. Arthur Dunkel, who was later director general of GATT, chaired the negotiations, and those negotiations—perhaps because others in the government wanted no part of them—were left largely to the Department of Agriculture. I know this created a great deal of frustration for Al McDonald because the European Community kept coming to him and saying, If you don't get Hathaway to do the right things, we will not move on anything else. Al would promptly invite me to one of his dinners or breakfasts, and I would explain to him why I wouldn't do that. We had a number of conversations.

In essence, those negotiations were finally terminated on two counts. First, it became perfectly obvious that the European Community wanted a world stabilization system in which they never put up any money and had relatively few obligations. Second, some of the other major exporters, especially Australia, said forget it, because we are going to need special exceptions. So the grains negotiation came to a close and we finally ended up with a relatively modest tariff agreement in agriculture. Ambassador Strauss and Ambassador McDonald spent hours trying to get some control of European export subsidies.

The result turned out in fact to be no control over export subsidies at all. It had no real effect, as we found out later, and it was not until the Uruguay Round that some effective control over European export subsidies were finally established. So in general the Tokyo Round was a fairly modest achievement at best for agriculture. But we avoided some of the worst difficulties. My own view has always been that if we had signed the grains agreement it would have collapsed in 1982. Probably some other things would have collapsed with it. We avoided that disaster, made modest access gains, and had general support in the agricultural establishment for passage at the end. There were a few exceptions, such as opposition in the dairy industry.

Eckes: Secretary Hathaway, I am puzzled by your comment that in agriculture the Tokyo Round was a "modest achievement." A pamphlet prepared in STR on the Tokyo Round of Multilateral Trade Negotiations says, "In the opinion of the Carter administration agriculture has been one of the big winners in the Tokyo Round."[2] [laughter]

Hathaway: Ask Alan Wolff about that—I didn't write it.

McDonald: Agriculture gave so little! Actually on agriculture we were fighting a defensive battle. We had almost nothing to negotiate with, as I remember. The most embarrassing question that I got was, What do you have in agriculture that you are willing to give? I was in constant contact with Dale [Hathaway], asking,

Don't we have something to give? We finally came up with 15,000 tons of cheese, and the wine gallon issue. We got the most we could out of the wine gallon concession. That was about it. It was an extraordinarily sensitive issue, and the fact that we were even discussing agriculture was a breakthrough, because there was always the concern, Should we be discussing this issue? In the political arena we had some of our best support from agricultural sources. The California community was solidly with us all the way. We got major concessions to benefit the almond trade, as one example.

One important gain involved rice. The chairman of the Senate Finance Committee [Russell Long] came from Louisiana, which was a big rice-growing state. We were able to obtain some concessions on rice and that was not disadvantageous. Later I was invited down as a hero to one of their association meetings to proclaim what we had accomplished. The gains were modest but at least they were steps in the right direction. At least the Tokyo Round set a precedent for discussing agricultural subjects in the GATT.

Eckes: Let's turn our discussion to the subject of nontariff barriers, where much was done that hadn't been attempted in previous GATT negotiations. Perhaps a good place to begin is with the subsidies code. Gary Hufbauer was actively involved in these negotiations.

Gary Hufbauer: Treasury's responsibility for this subject derived from Treasury's administration of the countervailing duty law, which of course changed at the end of the round. Both Secretary Mike Blumenthal and Assistant Secretary Fred Bergsten were very keen on bringing down the level of subsidies. Their analysis was that the United States would never be able politically to spend as much as other countries. Therefore we had to negotiate them down. That was the general framework.

In this policy area our approach was quite different from the military arms policy pursued to end the Cold War. There we outspent the Soviet Union and destroyed them. In subsidies we were never going to outspend anybody, not in agriculture, industry, or anything else. So it was clearly a subject for negotiations. The one subsidy we had at the time of any significance at the federal level was the DISC, thought by some to rank among the great contributions to mankind!

The Treasury was always divided on the DISC issue. There were those on the legal side who thought it was quite a good innovation. Most of the economists didn't think it was so good. But the balance clearly shifted when President Carter was elected, because he cited it as one of the abominations of mankind. Carter's dislike was perhaps a bit strong because DISC was a relatively small provision. But he clearly did not like it, and that put it on the [negotiating] table. The U.S. had lost a GATT case on this issue, where the core question was tax deferral via the DISC—that is, you pay your taxes later—and other countries, particularly the European Community, including France and other constituent members, were very concerned that deferral would turn into forgiveness. They were right. When DISC was eliminated, deferral did turn into forgiveness. That was about an $8 billion item.

On the European side, EC member countries had lost in the same set of GATT decisions—over the absence of any arms-length pricing and therefore domestic taxation on their exports. So we both had won and lost in the legal case that preceded the discussions.

I should mention that export credits were very much on the table at the same time even though the forum was somewhat different. It was the OECD export credit consensus group—a gentleman's agreement. This was another area where the United States thought it would never be able to spend as much as other countries.

Al McDonald and others have mentioned the importance of negotiating partnerships. In this area the key partner was Peter Klein, the European negotiator, but Rodney Grey of Canada was also terribly important. Klein spanned both negotiations, as I did, and Rodney, as ambassador from Canada, was very active on the subsidies side.

Let me offer a perspective on this issue of subsidies. I looked at some of the newspaper clippings sent to members of our panel, and it seems that this matter received a lot more attention than it really deserved. Perhaps it deserved the attention from an economic standpoint, because subsequent research has shown that small differences in tax rates over a period of time can make a big difference in investment location—and very likely make a bigger difference now than when we were negotiating, twenty years ago. The response rate technically is about twice as high as it was. So in a sense we were involved with an issue that made a difference. However, as a political issue, subsidies are not nearly as important now—or subsequent to the Tokyo Round—as they seemed in the run-up to the round. I will come back to that point in a moment.

Let me say something now about success or failure. The success, such as it was, of the subsidy code, and the complementary OECD agreement, was to sharply reduce export subsidies in areas other than agriculture. Agricultural subsidies were always off the table. Export subsides are not really a big issue today—by that I mean subsidies that specifically target exports for shipment to foreign markets. These are small items today, even in the export credit area. The failure was that the code did not then, and even the Uruguay Round version does not now, do much to limit investment subsidies, where there is no evident distinction between shipments abroad and shipments at home. These are subsidies designed to attract investments, and they do attract investments.

Let me comment on the political reasons why the outcome of the code was not so decisive as it might have seemed then and why the investment subsidies are so important. They tie together. First, a lot of investment subsidies have moved to the subfederal level in all countries. That subject was outside of any international negotiation in the Tokyo Round, and in the subsequent Uruguay Round. If you read the fine text of the Uruguay Round, the negotiators were not able to restrict effectively subfederal subsidies.

Second, in the years since the Tokyo Round there has been a huge shift in the way countries regard foreign direct investment. At the time we were negotiating, foreign direct investment was considered something alien—not entirely welcome. Well, the atmosphere has changed totally throughout the world on this issue in the last twenty years, and now foreign investment is welcome in practically every country and every sector. There are some reservations, but very few. What that means is that foreign firms are often quite happy to receive subsidies, tax incentives, and so forth. They have no reason to mount any legal or political campaign against those subsidies. That is why the political component turned out, in my judgment, to be very much less important in retrospect than in prospect.

Greenwald: I have a completely different recollection of, and view of, the outcome of the subsidies-countervailing duty negotiations. To begin with, the reason it was a central part of the negotiations was because every single negotiating partner was insisting that we include an injury standard in our countervailing duty law. So the dynamic was the insistence by other nations that we change our law. We had no good defense against that, and so our best defense became offense.

We decided what we were going to do: we were going to try to introduce discipline on subsidies, nominally, if not in real terms. That in turn raised enormous difficulties for the rest of the world. Not because it was a tax issue. Actually, the DISC and differences in various other Treasury-financed tax subsidies were not the driving forces. The issue was millions and millions of dollars being funneled to British Steel and the rest of European steel, and overt export subsidies in developing countries like India, where the textile industry would receive enormous incentives—15 or 20 percent—to export rather than to sell for domestic consumption. The political difficulty was that while we were willing to change our countervailing duty laws, it became a very sensitive issue when one talked about reducing the British government's ability to funnel however many billions it wanted to British Steel, or changing an export promotion scheme in India or Brazil or wherever. The fact is that fundamental changes in subsidy practices overseas were not then—and I do not believe are now—negotiable in the sense that they will become subject to effective international discipline.

What happened in fact was a code, which promised far more than it could deliver, and an awareness among U.S. negotiators that the real payoff, if you will, for the domestic constituency did not lie in the discipline that would flow from an international regime over subsidies. Rather it was in the promise that implementing legislation held for aggressive use of countervailing duty laws. Without the material injury standard, U.S. law was something of an embarrassment and was not used. In fact, after implementation of the Tokyo Round agreement on subsidies and countervailing duties, steel and other industries began for the first time to use U.S. countervailing duty law, with a very low injury threshold, as a weapon against foreign use of subsidies. And this may have led to some discipline—certainly more discipline than flowed from the international code—on use of subsidies by the British government and the French government to finance their overseas export industries.

McDonald: A word on the negotiation of these codes. This is a perfect illustration of the way we tried to work together as a team. We went as far as we could at Geneva with our team, and we had two very dedicated people, at least, who were working on the subsidies and countervailing duties. One was our deputy head of delegation, Bill Culbert, but he had reached a point of impasse with the Geneva representative for the EEC, Paul Luyten. It was almost impossible for them to be in the same room. So that was not going far. . . . We really had to call up reinforcements, and I called on Dick Rivers. He and John Greenwald spent more time than they ever envisaged thinking they were part of the Washington team, when really they became part of the Geneva negotiating team.

It was clear from the outset, from my point of view, that the DISC had to go. We had to get something to counterbalance that, and we had to get some latitude. I commend Dick and John for the fine job they did. It was a great relief to have their help along the way.

Greenwald: I wish there had been more to the final agreement. [laughter]

Wolff: I think both Gary and John are right. The legitimacy of use of countervailing duty law was very important to the United States. I don't think the [public relations] materials that came out when the agreements went to the Hill sold it that way, but the fact is we could not impose countervailing duties without it causing a major trade conflict as long as the United States did not have an injury test. Once we had an injury test, we could and did impose countervailing duties. It made that part of the law useful, and it was an important gain, although it was not what we were seeking. It was what other nations were seeking.

On the prohibition of subsidies, it is very difficult to assess a negative. There was a prohibition which was allegedly enforceable under the international agreement. In the United States it is taken seriously when something would infringe our international commitments, especially when there might be a right of action against us when we make policy decisions. To the extent that there was prohibition in the Tokyo Round agreement, one would need to discuss this with a panel of representatives of foreign governments to understand how much we affected their practices. I do agree with both John and Gary that the fundamental domestic subsidies could not be reached at the time and really have not been reached since.

McDonald: One additional comment on the business point of view: Subsidies are always of great concern and of great political interest to industrial and business groups. Whenever we face a subsidy, in reality we go into a private negotiation and usually we can negotiate some sort of counterconcession of a local sort—the movement of funds, investment returns, or something else. So even though it is not as clean as it should be, I think the code has helped us in private negotiations in this regard.

Eckes: Are there any comments on the antidumping code?

S. Bruce Wilson: I would like to add something on the subsidies issue. One of the objectives of the rest of the world vis-à-vis the United States was to get a countervailing injury test under U.S. law. When we implemented this agreement under U.S. law, there was a debate within the U.S. government as to who should get that injury test—whether only signatories of the code should get the injury test or not.

When we followed up on implementation of this code, we had real problems because there were only a few developing countries which signed the code. I think the administration had flexibility as to whether or not to apply the injury test. After the agreements were implemented in 1980, we had real problems with a number of developing countries because they did not sign the code and we did not give them an injury test. We tried to negotiate bilateral commitments from them so that they would be eligible for the injury test. Subsequently, India—after we signed a bilateral agreement and did not follow through—took us to the GATT and alleged that we violated most favored nation, because we did not give them an injury test while we gave it to others who signed. Ultimately, we resolved that matter bilaterally, but it was a residual problem of the Tokyo Round that proved to be a very difficult management problem. The implementation of this agreement proved very problematic regarding the developing countries for a number of years.

Hufbauer: We had a huge debate within the Treasury Department about the conditional versus the unconditional most favored nation approach. There were very strong academic experts who urged unconditional MFN. I think the strongest intellectually was Professor John Jackson [University of Michigan]. In the Treasury we came to the view that the unconditional approach was a dead-end approach, and that we had to go the conditional route here and elsewhere in order to drag these laggard countries into the party. I think we won that debate and it flowed over into our approach toward regionalism. I don't think other countries would have come in to the subsidies code agreement if they had seen that we were wedded to unconditional MFN as a matter of faith. I think that was as important a result of the subsidies code as some of the other issues which were on the political forefront at the time.

Greenwald: The comment suggests that the real importance of the Tokyo Round in these areas is the international agreement on subsidies, and I would suggest that is nonsense. In fact, the international agreements are of relatively minor significance. However, one of the real lasting impacts of the Tokyo Round was to funnel sensitive domestic industry actions against disruptive imports into the countervailing duty and antidumping statutes. And that was a deliberate part of the negotiating strategy which kept an eye to the implementing process while international agreements were being structured, so that the law that followed from the agreement gave the United States enough flexibility to make the law into a pretty effective instrument for industries like steel. Incidentally, the changes to the antidumping law were more significant than the countervailing duty laws. One of things that should surprise anyone reading this transcript is the fact that the steel industry was one of the strongest supporters of the Tokyo Round. There is only one reason for it. They knew full well that their best defenses against subsidies, dumping, and other disruptive trade practices were through unilateral U.S. use of our trade statutes. To me that is one of the most important and lasting legacies of the Tokyo Round that was spawned by, but was not really part of, the international negotiating process.

Kelly: Bruce Wilson mentioned that there were a lot of residual problems in the GATT that had to be dealt with at the end of the Tokyo Round. I was working in the GATT in 1980. I can tell you that the biggest residual problem we had was the one Bruce described on subsidies—not only with regard to the MFN problem but others as well. I would like to congratulate Mr. Wilson who negotiated these difficult bilateral agreements with regard to MFN.

Eckes: Let's move to the procurement code. If one looks at statements U.S. officials made to Congress after the round concluded, the procurement code seemed to loom very large among the benefits. How does the procurement code look from today's perspective? [silence]

Amy Porges: The procurement code actually does give one of the few examples of the use of conditional MFN as effective leverage. I think it is true that the conditional MFN approach in the subsidies code proved very difficult to implement. In the first years I worked at STR, I spent much of my time working on developing country export subsidies with relatively little return. Except, of course, when the country concerned was under pressure of a countervailing duty suit. In such cases they were quick to try to negotiate a deal temporarily to limit their export subsidies, join the code, and break the deal the following year. . . . The U.S. implemented the procurement code in an interesting way. The U.S. essentially tried to bar nonmembers of the code from all of the code-covered procurement, and eventually the U.S. took the same approach to Uruguay Round code. In fact it was that approach that eventually forced Singapore and

Hong Kong, I think, to join the new code and not stick with the Tokyo Round. That was effective leverage.

McDonald: I would like to comment on this one. There were two aspects. For those of us who were negotiating, we had assumed that we would not necessarily open our markets to nonsigners. We said that specifically—I was adamant—in the Geneva discussions. At the same time we had many opposite views in our government. I received a State Department memorandum saying that we are not sure that it is the policy we want to follow. We in the U.S. are also a consuming country. We really do want the best product at the cheapest price. Although we like it to be bought American, we prefer the lowest price and the best quality. Therefore, there was really no way we could close off American purchases at the state and local level, as well as the federal level. So anything we could get would be a plus for us.

The second comment I would make as a business person having spent more than ten years in Europe prior to that time. We were not so much interested in selling to the government as a government institution, but we were much interested in selling to government-controlled institutions and companies. When we looked at France, for example, something like 50 percent of the GNP was controlled by nationalized companies. We were essentially barred from most of those until after the code was in place. These [lost opportunities] don't get into the government records because they were not official. But if you look at the proliferation of U.S. products sold to nationalized companies afterwards, there was a major movement. Those of us on the business side saw this as a real opportunity. To illustrate, selling the department of education in France was not a very attractive opportunity, but selling Air France, which I was doing, was. Selling to the French steel and aircraft industries was very important.

I would submit that when you look at the government situation we faced a de facto opening of the U.S. market under any circumstance, except what was covered by buy-America statutes. We wanted to open the secondary market so that government-controlled institutions would find it politically acceptable to deal with us. This was a substantial market. If we look back at it now, we would find that American companies and American producers have gained major customers—particularly among units that were earlier nationalized.

So there are several aspects to the procurement code. There is another thing—while only twelve entities signed initially, that understates its importance. There are now twelve countries in the European Community, although that counted as only one of the signing entities. From the standpoint of the negotiations, we considered the matter in terms of the percentage of world trade covered, not in terms of the number of countries signing. From that perspective we had between two-thirds and 70 percent of world trade covered by countries that really could afford to buy substantially abroad. That is what counted from a business perspective.

Fox: Mr. McDonald is absolutely right. When you take the trend toward privatization which has taken place, the Bundespost [federal postal system] was always a marvelous objective, but you could never sell anything to them while they were part of the German government. This privatization business really makes a big difference, and it does not show up in the data because they are not government entities.

Eckes: One of the major problems was access to the Japanese telecommunications market, and the Japanese were stubbornly resistant, and U.S. negotiators gained relatively little. Is that correct?

Katz: I don't recall specifically what we got in that negotiation, but there was a subsequent bilateral negotiation on NTT [Nippon Telephone and Telegraph] where the U.S. government got substantial access.

McDonald: There was a long negotiation when I was at the White House and it went on for a year or two. I think had it not been for the government procurement code that negotiation would not have occurred. The code provided a solid justification to open up the discussion. Since that time—and over the last ten years I have served on the board of a major high-tech company, and frankly Japan has been one of our better markets. . . . Sometimes it is very hard to measure what is a direct impact and what is an indirect one.

Katz: I think the significance of the procurement code is less in what it achieved at that particular moment. The breakthrough in terms of an approach to procurement subsequently provided successes in subsequent negotiations.

Wilson: What Jules has said is correct. The procurement code was the first time that this area had been subject to international rules. This is a long-term process. I remember that the notion was that we would expand the coverage under the procurement code after three years of operation. Of course, the coverage of the procurement code was not expanded until we did the Uruguay Round, some fifteen years later. I think the matter has to be looked at in a long time frame.

The other part of the procurement code that was really indicative of what was happening in the Tokyo Round as a whole with respect to nontariff measures is that there was very little developing-country participation. The briefing materials bring this out. For all of these groundbreaking agreements, they were largely agreements among developed countries. The negotiations were conducted primarily between the developed countries, starting with the U.S. and the European Communities. Then we expanded the circle to include Japan, Canada, and other developed countries. The developing countries were not really brought into the negotiating process until the end of the day—and the result was there was little developing-country participation in these agreements. I also think the legacy of this was that when we went into the subsequent round [Uruguay Round] there was a decision made by U.S. policymakers that we had to approach that round as a single undertaking by virtue of the fact that in our estimation the developing countries had pretty much gotten a free ride in the Tokyo Round.

Now, the developing countries didn't look at it that way. They thought the tariff concessions we had made on products of interest to them in the Tokyo Round had been rather modest and therefore did not justify their participation in some of these nontariff measure agreements. The overall outcome of the nontariff negotiations in terms of getting developing-country participation was rather slender. With respect to the NTT situation, I was not involved in that negotiation, Doug Newkirk was. But it is my recollection that we told the Japanese that we would not apply the government procurement code to them unless they agreed to a negotiated settlement on NTT. So, whatever you think about the results of the NTT agreement—and I think the assessment of that agreement has been mixed over time—it was not possible until we had the procurement code in place to use that as a lever vis-à-vis the Japanese.

Porges: Exactly. As you may recall, the procurement code was not finished until 1981—not 1980—and the NTT problem delayed it. Under the reciprocity clause in the Trade Agreements Act of 1979, the U.S. refused to apply to the procurement code to Japan until the NTT issue was settled. The way it was settled is interesting. It went from an offer of coverage—the Japanese started by only agreeing to cover under the procurement code itself those things that were not included in the provision of public telecommunication services—telephone poles, concrete telephone poles. The U.S. rightly wanted more, a more meaningful agreement. The deal that was done was not to cover that other stuff under the code but to cover it bilaterally under a U.S.-Japan agreement, which was essentially a parallel procurement code with special rules that were supposed to solve the Japan problem. That problem was elaborated upon in two or three renewals. I am sure the other people at this table have views on whether those rules have been effective in solving the Japan problem.

Wolff: I think it is important to go back to the notion of a continuum. Tariffs really had been the only successful subject of multilateral negotiations prior to the Tokyo Round. After the Kennedy Round, Congress rejected the American selling price agreement. The 1967 antidumping code also did not appeal to Congress. Through adoption of the fast-track process in 1974, the U.S. developed the means internally of agreeing to international understandings that affected matters beyond tariffs. We also got other nations accustomed to dealing with nontariff measures as well.

These nontariff codes were groundbreaking. Each one of these codes opened up new areas and made them legitimate for international consideration, without which a services agreement in the Uruguay Round would not have been possible. One could not have jumped from the Kennedy Round immediately into issues such as the right of establishment and the full participation of developing countries. I am sure that when China accedes to the WTO, we will address a problem that Al McDonald alluded to: state-invested enterprises in a nonmarket or mixed economy. None of this would be possible without some steppingstones along the way, and the Tokyo Round provided an important series of steppingstones.

Eckes: During the symposium on the Kennedy Round we heard much about the role of GATT director general Wyndham White. In our discussion today we have not touched on the actions of senior GATT officials in the Tokyo Round. What roles did Director General Olivier Long and Arthur Dunkel play in helping to reach a final agreement?

McDonald: I don't think it was very significant. We saw Long on formal social occasions and formal meetings, but he was not actively involved in the negotiations, nor was he a factor. His successor, Arthur Dunkel, was. One of the interesting things when you are negotiating as a member of the American business community or government is that whether it is by envy, jealously, or resentment we are not often welcome as the thought leaders in foreign negotiations. The United States is envied and admired but also feared because of its great commercial weight. It is often a political plus for other nations to oppose or undermine U.S. trade proposals.

Therefore, we have to go back to Benjamin Franklin's view that anytime I want to get an idea across, I need someone to advocate it for me who is perceived as somewhat more neutral. Arthur Dunkel played a key role here as head of the Swiss delegation—and his associate, Carlo Jagmetti, until recently the ambassador in Washington, who left under not the most auspicious circumstances. They were highly instrumental in aiding the major parties to reconcile our differences. We spent many quiet dinners—with five or six or eight or ten—heads of developing country delegations informally scouting what could be done in each of the negotiating areas. We were much concerned about the material that was submitted to the GATT, because the organization had two deputy directors—one representing the LDCs.

Anything that went into the GATT went immediately to the LDCs. It triggered immediate opposition. We had enough trouble trying to deal with nations representing a majority of the world's trade.

[Among the LDCs] there was strictly a desire to have a one-way street. One of the things we tried to do in the codes was to insist that those who didn't sign wouldn't get the privileges. But we also knew that Americans are generous people and probably in the implementation that position might not hold. At least our Geneva position was a lever . . . But the GATT served as a formal meeting ground to announce what we had already agreed to. I do not recall a single active negotiating session under the auspices of the GATT.

Eckes: That would seem to be different from the Kennedy Round and the Uruguay Round,

Katz: There was a very great difference between the performance of Eric Wyndham White on the one hand and Olivier Long on the other. Part of it was personality, part of it was also circumstance. Wyndham White's tenure as director general was at a time when you had a much smaller group of countries—more like-minded, although there were some developing countries, such as Brazil and India—but they didn't play a major role. At the time of the Tokyo Round you had ninety-nine countries, compared to perhaps fifty countries in the Kennedy Round and a handful in the initial rounds. The scale of the effort was much different. Eric Wyndham White was much more participatory. He chaired meetings in his little office, the old headquarters of the GATT.

As far as Arthur Dunkel's role in the Uruguay Round, he was certainly active but I would say he was less than totally effective. The greatest thing he ever did was to put together and put out the Dunkel Report at the end of 1991, which was important, because it was a catalytic event pulling together all the elements of the negotiations and laying them out. As soon as it was criticized—heavily by the European Community—he ran away from it. [The criticism] was not for lack of effort. He was not as effective as I think he might have been had he taken stronger stands at critical points.

Hufbauer: I want to return to the previous topic. The great success with developing countries in the Uruguay Round really was made possible by a fundamental shift in their economic policies—open markets, privatization, and changes in internal policies—which really had nothing to do with trade negotiations. In my view, negotiations can make the last 25 percent of the difference, but the 75 percent had to be there from internal economic policies, or it was not possible. And that is what has always been lacking with Japan and some of the other East Asian countries, including India. When the Japanese banks finally collapse, Japan may be ready to liberalize, but during this whole period of time the basis has not been there with Japan. It did come with Brazil and with Mexico.

McDonald: If I can comment for a minute on the LDCs, I think Jules' point is a critical one. There had been an explosion of national entities in the years preceding the Tokyo Round. Many of these countries were impoverished and struggling for existence. They were looking for a totally free ride.

I spent more time than I would like to think with the LDCs discussing issues and their concerns. We tried to introduce the idea of graduation. I spent a long time with George Alvares Maciel, the ambassador from Brazil, for example, and the ambassador from India [Prem Kumar], because if you couldn't persuade those two, you didn't have a hope of bringing along some of the others. They could understand our position, but politically they were in no position to go along with what we were asking for in the codes.

There was an issue of sovereignty. We were not simply talking about tariffs. For the first time in a multilateral negotiation we were saying, We think you should submit to an international body, at least for discussion purposes, things that have previously been held as the sole prerogative of sovereign nations. Each one of the codes impinges on that sovereignty. This was something they simply were not capable of supporting with their own internal political structures at the time, which were highly protective and nationalistic. They all wanted the benefits of the Tokyo Round, but they wanted essentially no obligations. That was the reality of the case. We did pursue each one on the tariff side, which was the only area in which we could progress. I remember that Martin Smith, who is sitting in the back here, was one of the junior members of the delegation, working with Harvey Bale. He was assigned to Pakistan and he successfully ended up with a tariff agreement in which we made certain concessions on both sides.

Porges: Let me briefly ask Bruce Wilson about the valuation code. I think that code got the widest participation among LDCs. How did you achieve that?

Wilson: The customs valuation agreement had been negotiated primarily among the developed countries. The U.S. and the European Community had come to an agreement on the content of that code. As one who led the Washington team on that negotiation, I remember going to Geneva twelve times in nine months. Most of the substantive negotiations were done in 1978. At the end of that negotiation, all of the developing countries had said they were not going to adhere to it. I remember that we were struggling with how to get the developing countries on board.

While we were going through the implementing process here legislatively with Congress in the early part of 1979, we made another try with the developing countries in Geneva on some agreements, including customs valuation. Over the course of several months we negotiated a protocol to the valuation agreement which picked up on the idea of graduation, which would allow the developing countries to take five years to implement the obligations of the valuation agreement. At the same time, from the outset they would receive full membership in the agreement. As you said, from the U.S. perspective these agreements were always envisaged to be self-contained, self-governing agreements. So we negotiated a protocol to the valuation agreement and concluded that in the spring of 1979. We were thus able to get India, Brazil, Korea, and Argentina on the basis of that protocol negotiation to adhere to the valuation agreement. We thought that was a pretty good outcome, for it set the stage over time for more developing countries to come into that particular agreement.

Eckes: As our session moves to a close, it is appropriate to turn to the big-picture question—the question of the Tokyo Round's significance in comparison with other GATT rounds. How does the Tokyo Round look after twenty years? If you had it to do over again, what would you do differently? How do you assess your efforts?

Kelly: I would like to go back first. One of the reasons why the subsidy code got such big attention was Danish butter cookies, which is how we started on this subsidy road. When Bob Strauss came in, one of the biggest problems he had with the European Community was Denmark and imports of subsidized butter cookies.

Another comment, following up on Jules' remarks, about the precedential nature of these codes: In the GATT it says that government procurement is specifically outside the provisions of GATT—and this was at U.S. insistence in 1947, when it was negotiated. So it was a major change to have negotiations on government procurement.

And in regard to the customs valuation code it is important to remember the controversy over American selling price. Congress did not accept an agreement negotiated in the Kennedy Round to phase out ASP. The issue became a sine qua non for the Tokyo Round. The United States was under pressure to do something about ASP. The problem of congressional approval led to the fast-track provision in the legislation providing us with authority for the Tokyo Round. In the Kennedy Round agreement there was a provision saying that if we ever got rid of ASP, we reserved the right to convert the tariffs on benzenoid chemicals, based on ASP, to their ad valorem equivalents.

This proved quite an exercise! The ISACs were a great help, because who knows what the ad valorem equivalent is on yellow dye no. 13? In making these conversions to ad valorem equivalents we were on the telephone with the chemical ISACs all the time trying to figure out the appropriate rates. Not only did we convert to ad valorem equivalents, but we also cut these rates by up to 50 percent.

Rubber footwear was another item involved in this conversion. I remember when we converted that rate to 65 percent. Wilbur Mills had said earlier he would never agree to this, but Wilbur Mills was no longer around.

Let me make a few more comments about tariffs. One of the things that the industry advisers liked in the legislation was the opportunity we had to convert specific and compound rates of duty to ad valorem equivalents. Over the years a specific rate of duty (ten cents per quantity) becomes less protective. We did a massive conversion of specific to ad valorem equivalents, and this was very helpful in selling the Tokyo Round to the private sector.

We had some problems in the pottery area—involving stoneware. Senator Jennings Randolph had some stoneware producers in West Virginia. Others were along the Ohio River in Pennsylvania. We had the authority in the legislation to raise duties in this negotiation. We actually raised duties on stoneware and this made a few people very grateful. But, we cut the duties on fine china by 50 percent. That was the way we got the Japanese and others to agree to the raising of the duties on stoneware. The Japanese and the others figured they were going to move into the higher-value china anyway, so they were able to stomach the increased duties on stoneware.

Then we have the truck issue. Everyone says tariffs are not important. At the end of the negotiation we still had a 25-percent duty on trucks that was not touched. The truck duty just happened to catch some vans that entered the country as well. The automobile industry liked the agreement very much since it kept the 25-percent rate of duty.

On textiles, we did very little. The European Community pressed us on textiles and particularly on apparel, such as boys wool suits. We developed the "elevator," whereby if the European Community would cut on such and such, we would cut on such and such. The EC did not want to cut on anything, so we cut very little. On ceramic tile, another difficult problem, we made minimal or no cuts. That was also true for leather goods.

So we were able to preserve some of our high tariffs, which were good selling points on the Hill when it came time to present this package to Congress.

McDonald: Let me comment on that. One of the big differences, as I understand it, was that the Kennedy Round operated on a formula in tariff negotiations. In contrast, we operated on an item-by-item basis. Now you can imagine the complexity of that change. It required real expertise from our industrial groups on what we should achieve. But it also increased the amount of work in the negotiations exponentially because each item was really important.

Before we leave all the codes let me say one thing about the standards code and the customs valuation code. When you do business every day, these are frankly more important than some of the others, because standards can be one of the quickest ways to bar an importer from a country, or customs valuation can change one's whole economics overnight. So although these were not so attractive in terms of major policy movements from a strictly governmental point of view, from a pragmatic business point of view they were clearly steps in the right direction and helped to lower the risk level of investments, to expand international commercial business.

Greenwald: Let me go back to the bottom-line question, assessing the Tokyo Round, and say something that may invite comment. What grade should we give ourselves twenty years later? My guess is a D– or maybe F+. First, let me say where the "+" on the F comes from. I think that fast track is a lasting contribution, not a function of negotiations but a unique negotiating authority, and it has shaped U.S. trade policy since. But the F part comes from whether or not the negotiations as a whole were fighting the right war and whether we addressed the right issues. I think it very clear when you look back, what you have, and had, is a Japan problem unresolved, an Asian problem generally unresolved—such as Korea. One of the things that struck me recently was realizing that the Korean tariff on automobiles was never bound. More generally, there was an unresolved less-developed-country problem. Finally, if you look at Europe, the focus of our effort, there is also little to show. Agriculture was unsolved. We didn't get much on Euro-telecom. We didn't get much on Airbus, or on industrial policy generally.

Over the last twenty years the changes have been much more the result of political developments within Europe than anything that was negotiated. I think that any fair analysis—not of pottery versus fine china, but of the fundamental issues that were out there waiting for resolution—leads to the conclusion that they were not resolved.

There are two other points I would like to make. What about the notion that the codes that were agreed to were groundbreaking? I agree with that. But there is also a conceit involved that is terribly dangerous. The conceit is that in nontariff barriers, codes of international conduct are sufficient disciplines in and of themselves on behavior. When the Uruguay Round came around—and I view the Tokyo Round as a halfway point to the Uruguay Round—there was a feeling that the codes themselves were sufficiently strong to discipline, or channel, behavior. Thus, we could have a multilateral dispute settlement process that abandoned U.S. unilateral authority to address problems that the codes in fact proved powerless to address.

One of the saving graces of the Tokyo Round was dispute settlement, which no one has mentioned. The United States took the lead in trying to establish what we would call a tougher international discipline over trade disputes. The idea of tougher international discipline may strike many as a contradiction of terms. Be that as it may, the U.S. pushed for that, and we were perfectly willing to have sort of final-say automaticity in the system that was agreed to in the Uruguay Round.

The Europeans opposed it—Paul Luyten, in particular, felt that surrender of political muscle in trade disputes was a terrible mistake. In retrospect, I think he was right. But even on that point I think you have to view the Tokyo Round as a steppingstone to the Uruguay Round, where the international dispute settlement process was multilateralized. Again, it leaves you with the conceit that international codes and conduct are going to end up being effective measures for disciplining international trade behavior.

Hufbauer: Well, once again John and I disagree. It is like old times. I think the grade is much more a B+, and the reason it isn't an A– is the laundry list of shortcomings we've heard. The reason that it is as high as a B+ is, if you take the developments of the last twenty years, trade has grown 2 to 4 percent per year higher than GDP. Not all of that can be attributed to liberalization. About half of that can be attributed to rapidly falling interconnection costs—telecoms, airlines, transportation, and so forth. But, with all the trade barriers coming down, the Tokyo Round was still a milestone.

More importantly, I think you just have to look around today . . . and contrast the financial system with the trading system. When you do so, you must give this agreement a very high grade. By that I mean the fine degree of articulation, and the creation of bodies of people in corporations and government who know these rules and look after them, self-enforce the trading system to a very large degree. This institutionalization really kept the trading system working in the 1970s crisis, during the difficult period of the high dollar in the 1980s, and now in the wake of the Asia crisis from deteriorating very much.

When you contrast that with the financial system, which totally lacks this degree of surveillance, the difference is striking. When you look at what the BIS [Bank for International Settlements] has done, or the IMF, you find a big zero. A lot of talk and big zeros in terms of real surveillance. By comparison, I think the trading system comes off extremely well, and the Tokyo Round was part of the success.

Wolff: John [Greenwald] makes it very hard to agree with him. John goes beyond whether the glass is half full and finds it difficult to see whether it has any moisture in it at all. John finds it difficult to find where the benefits were. We live in a world that is very imperfect, but it is a world that the trade agreements program, the GATT, and the WTO have contributed to enormously. There is still important work to be done. One of the missing elements relates to Japanese structural barriers.

On the significance of the Tokyo Round, first we should not forget that Congress had never approved a trade agreement negotiated by the executive unless the Congress had given advance authority. There was an automotive agreement in which authority was given. But the Russian trade agreement and the nontariff agreements from the Kennedy Round went down to defeat. So the executive and Congress formed a partnership, and this brought about a dramatic grant of authority [Trade Act of 1974]. This was an extraordinary accomplishment.

The Tokyo Round proved that partnership could work, and it did work. It worked extraordinarily well. It was created for this purpose and the trust was taken and exercised and the results were approved. And, as Bob Strauss said, it was hardly mentioned in the *Washington Post* because it was a nonevent, it was not contentious by the time it happened. This was a stroke of political mastery.

Another thing that the Tokyo Round established was the legitimacy of the GATT itself. Before the 1974 Trade Act the GATT was not mentioned in U.S. law. The 1974 Trade Act mentioned it with some neutrality, and in the 1979 act it was mentioned throughout.

I too worry about some of the directions that are being taken in the future in the WTO and I am concerned with its inadequacies, but the fact is the government of the U.S.—including the Congress—for the first time in 1979 recognized the legitimacy of an international trade organization. Where I agree very substantially with John is that the whole package has to be looked at—as we looked upon it at the time, and Congress did—as to what the U.S. was going to do with respect to implementation as well as what the agreements said. We had been totally unable to use countervailing duties. They had no legitimacy without an injury test and they became legitimate. They were transferred to two agencies that operated with sunshine procedures. These were the International Trade Commission and the Commerce Department.

Section 301 was put in the 1974 act and was thoroughly usable after the Tokyo Round was over. Import relief provisions (Section 201), were usable after several years of falling into disuse. That statute's use seems somewhat cyclical. We formed a partnership with the European Community which was extremely important and has largely lasted through most problems. No, we didn't cure the Airbus problem, but each one of the problems that were not cured have some idiosyncracies to it. If you went to Boeing at the time and said, Should we go to war over whether Europe has an aircraft industry, the answer was no. The answer was no from the Congress as well. One can only do what the domestic constituency allows you to do in most instances.

We established a process of consultation with the private sector that was extraordinarily successful and very beneficial. We didn't do it willingly. The Congress gave us that, and it worked. I have already spoken about nontariff measures. Without those earlier agreements, we would not have had very significant accomplishments on telecom and financial services in the present, which are making a difference. Access to the Japanese market in financial services was simply unthinkable a while earlier.

What failures were there? Some of the successes Bill Kelly listed could be viewed by others as failures. I have thought for years that we could we have done more in textiles. We could have done a textile agreement and still had domestic support, maybe with a few fewer votes. We could have said we are going to phase out restrictions over a generation—and it would have worked. It would actually have been about the same time frame as that ultimately used. In retrospect, it would have been a mistake to do it in the Tokyo Round. The Uruguay Round put to good use the textile negotiating leverage to deal with developing countries. In the Tokyo Round we paved the way for what followed. Most of it was very positive. The United States has had unprecedented growth, and open markets have meant an enormous amount to us.

The gentleman who opened our session, Robert Strauss, proved that individuals matter in a profound way, that the exercise of leadership, judgment, and political sense makes an enormous difference. He was once on Air Force One and Jimmy Carter said to him, "Look out the window at all the stars and heavens. Isn't that fascinating?" Most of us would have said, "Yes, sir." Strauss said, "I have no interest in that whatsoever. What I care about is people." He established lasting relationships with people he negotiated with. He knew he couldn't get more from them than they could deliver, and that defined the parameters of the negotiations. He taught us all quite a number of good lessons.

Katz: The Tokyo Round agreement, like all agreements, is described as historic. It needs to be put into a historical context. That is, it was an element of a policy that we have pursued now for nearly seventy years, designed to progressively reduce barriers to trade and to build a rule of law with respect to world trade. I think that we have been extraordinarily successful, although it has taken nearly seventy years to reach where we are now.

The Tokyo Round is but one element of that. It came at a particularly historic moment, which made it a transitional event. We were going from a system where we were negotiating primarily on tariffs on goods to something that was much broader. In the Kennedy Round we made the first attempt to deal with nontrade barriers, and it was pretty feeble and somewhat unsuccessful. Even what we negotiated, we could not deliver on. We could not carry out the agreements we had reached. In the Tokyo Round we had a new process for handling that, and while the agreements were imperfect—to put it mildly, they didn't go very far—they were groundbreaking. They were conceptual in many cases. They laid the basis for the further progress we made. And if you look at the total result where we are seventy years later—and where our economy is seventy years later—I think it is a historic step. I won't try to give it a letter grade.

Samuel: Let me respond to the question relating to the long-term impact of the Tokyo Round. Starting in the 1970s, many workers in the industrial sector, along with their unions, began to have doubts regarding the benefits of open trade—which were being heralded by assorted academics and some business leaders, even as their jobs were disappearing abroad. I suggest that the Tokyo Round fostered an even greater . . . disaffection and cynicism on the part of industrial workers, who could see very little benefit in the results and some damage, such as the implementation of the injury test in unfair trade cases.

This feeling of cynicism was probably exacerbated by what was perceived as the means of rounding up votes for the agreement, via special deals to key industries in order to assure their support. Other sectors, which were not awarded these deals (i.e., machinists, electrical workers) felt that their interests had been sacrificed in the process.

The hostility of much of labor to open trade, based on the belief that special interests usually trump the broad national interest, has not diminished since the Tokyo Round. Witness labor's battle against NAFTA and its opposition to an extension of fast track.

Since our national commitment to an open trade policy depends on broad public support, the alienation of many workers and their unions has been and probably will continue to be a major hindrance.

McDonald: I would certainly agree with Jules. I am also interested that we are discussing a commercial negotiation twenty years later. I work in a totally different sphere. I don't have any contract with any of my companies, that I know of, that exceeds ten years. In fact, I don't know of a strategy for any of them that has a life span of more than three or four years. The commercial world is a very dynamic one. I have been amused as a non-Beltway type to hear some of the reactions, because it all depends on what your measure is. Some of the measures I have heard used are policy measures of what are final solutions by governments. I submit in the course of human history there are very few final solutions in commercial relationships. You may find them in government but you will not find them in business. I don't think that you will find them in the commercial arena. We are all in the process of making small steps forward.

From my point of view, having been responsible overall for the negotiations, I could have saved John some trips to Geneva and a lot of agony at that point of time had I known how poorly he thought of the whole effort he was carrying out and what little impact it would have. [laughter] I would say the Tokyo Round changed the attitudes of a lot of people in business—and quite a few in government. I am extremely grateful, after being here today, that I chose to leave Washington when I left the White House and to go back into the commercial arena. I could not have lived productively in this environment for the last twenty years, I don't think, participating in policy arguments or discussions on whether we have come to final solutions or not. My patience level is not that high. I would rather be in real deals and expand trade. And probably the only contribution I could make to the Tokyo Round was trying to come up with a deal—the best commercial deal we could at that time.

But what I am reassured about is what has happened in the world economy and what has happened in international trade since then. I said the object of the game is to put as few barriers in the way [as possible] and to begin to reduce them as best you can. And I totally subscribe to Jules' point of view. This country has, since the days of Cordell Hull, pursued a path that was not very politically popular. And it was not politically popular when we were negotiating in Geneva on the Tokyo Round either. We are fundamentally a fairly inward-looking nation. We are relatively self-contained. We changed a lot of attitudes during the Tokyo Round and we opened a lot of ground that still offers an opportunity for advancement. The proportion of U.S. international trade [to GDP] has just about doubled, or more, since we were in Geneva twenty years ago. That is phenomenal change. I can assure you that the attitude of private business of taking risks to make investments across borders would be quite different if we had returned and said, We abort the whole thing, we cannot live in an international economy together, we have no hope. That is the other side of the question.

The Tokyo Round was only one step, but an important step. I think the Uruguay Round was another critical step forward. I hope that we continue with trade rounds about every decade because, if nothing else, we need to reassure the world that open trade is desirable and essential for global peace and prosperity.

I would like to make another comment. As Gary said, on the financial and economic side we have not made the progress that we have on trade. I have served on bank boards for more than a decade, and there is good reason for some of the difficulties we are having now. I regret to say I don't see an easy way out. But I wish we could think of some palliative. It wouldn't be a good policy solution, and it wouldn't satisfy John Greenwald's idea of success or final solution, but I surely wish we could put people's minds at peace some time soon so that we could continue to do business, make investments, and continue the path we have been on for the last few years.

I consider it a great privilege that Jules refused Bob Strauss's initial offer to go to Geneva and by some quirk of circumstances I happened to be making a speech in Tokyo that somebody heard, because I was not involved with government in any way at that time. Someone who heard me speak said to Bob Strauss, Here is a guy you ought to talk to. Initially, I thought he was asking my consulting firm to come in and do an assignment. I had no earthly idea he was asking me to quit a job that I had spent all my life trying to obtain. Nevertheless, it has been a great privilege to serve as head of the U.S. delegation in Geneva to complete the Tokyo Round of multilateral trade negotiations, particularly with this team represented here. I want to thank all of you for that opportunity and for your support during that tense time of negotiating uncertainty. It turned out to be one of the highlights of my career. Then, when I went back into the commercial side of the game, I felt a lot more comfortable in making investments, in putting my fortune into play, on a day-to-day basis in the international commercial sphere.

Hathaway: I think the Tokyo Round in agriculture marked a major turning point. I think it was at the end of the Tokyo Round that we recognized truly that there was no longer any value in pursuing what had been instrumental since the start of GATT, a policy of exempting agriculture from general rules relating to subsidies and similar practices. Therefore, the fact that we tried and failed to negotiate what I call the last gasp of expanding domestic programs to the rest of the world was a key thing that helped lay the groundwork for the Uruguay Round. In it we started to put agriculture back under the GATT. So, while the results in agriculture were pretty meager, I think they were instrumental in laying a groundwork for something far better in the Uruguay Round.

Eckes: In closing our discussion, I want to thank the participants for an extraordinarily stimulating session. I think students, scholars, and future trade negotiators will find the transcript of this session extremely valuable both in understanding the Tokyo Round and in addressing future commercial-policy problems.

NOTES

Preface

1. Clyde Prestowitz, *Trading Places* (New York: Basic Books, 1988), p. 259.

2. Among the books by participants, see John W. Evans, *The Kennedy Round in American Trade Policy: The Twilight of the GATT?* (Cambridge, Mass.: Harvard University Press, 1971); Ernest H. Preeg, *Traders and Diplomats: An Analysis of the Kennedy Round of Negotiations under the General Agreement on Tariffs and Trade* (Washington, D.C.: Brookings Institution, 1970).

Academic books on recent American trade policy include: Alfred E. Eckes, *Opening America's Market: U.S. Foreign Trade Policy since 1776* (Chapel Hill: University of North Carolina Press, 1995). On the Kennedy Round, see Thomas W. Zeiler, *American Trade and Power in the 1960s* (New York: Columbia University Press, 1992). Concerning the Tokyo Round, see William A. Lovett, Alfred E. Eckes Jr., and Richard L. Brinkman, *U.S. Trade Policy: History, Theory, and the WTO* (Armonk, N.Y.: M. E. Sharpe, 1999). On the origins of the GATT system, see Susan Aaronson, *Trade and the American Dream: A Social History of Postwar Trade Policy* (Lexington: University Press of Kentucky, 1996); Thomas W. Zeiler, *Free Trade, Free World: The Advent of GATT* (Chapel Hill: University of North Carolina Press, 1999).

Other scholarly works include I. M. Destler, *American Trade Politics: System under Stress* (New York: Twentieth Century Fund, 1986); Steve Dryden, *Trade Warriors: USTR and the American Crusade for Free Trade* (New York: Oxford University Press, 1995); Judith Goldstein, *Ideas, Interests, and American Trade Policy* (Ithaca: Cornell University Press, 1993); Robert A. Pastor, *Congress and the Politics of U.S. Foreign Economic Policy, 1929–1976* (Berkeley: University of California Press, 1980).

On the GATT system, see Patrick Low, *Trading Free: The GATT and U.S. Trade Policy* (New York: Twentieth Century Fund Press, 1993); Ernest H. Preeg, *Traders in a Brave New World: The Uruguay Round and the*

Future of the International Trading System (Chicago: University of Chicago Press, 1995); Gilbert R. Winham, *International Trade and the Tokyo Round Negotiation* (Princeton: Princeton University Press, 1986).

Among the standard legal interpretations, see Gerard Curzon, *Multilateral Commercial Diplomacy: The General Agreement on Tariffs and Trade and Its Impact on National Commercial Policies and Techniques* (London: Michael Joseph, 1965); Robert Hudec, *The GATT Legal System and World Trade Diplomacy* (New York: Praeger, 1975); John H. Jackson, *World Trade and the Law of GATT* (Charlottesville, Va.: Michie, 1969); John H. Jackson, *The World Trading System: Law and Policy of International Economic Relations* (Cambridge, Mass.: MIT Press, 1989); John H. Jackson and William J. Davey, *Legal Problems of International Economic Relations: Cases, Materials and Text,* 2d ed. (St. Paul, Minn.: West Publishing, 1986).

3. Sylvia K. Kraemer, "Policy Advisors: Historians and Making Policy," in *Public History: Essays from the Field,* ed. James B. Gardner and Peter S. LaPaglia (Malabar, Fla.: Krieger Publishing, 1999), pp. 217–28; quotes, pp. 224, 227.

Chapter One

1. Page numbers in parentheses indicate location of quotes in the following chapters.

2. *Public Papers of the Presidents [Lyndon B. Johnson] 1968* (Washington, D.C.: GPO, 1969), p. 199.

3. See generally Jackson, *World Trading System.* Legal scholars credit Jackson with inspiring the World Trade Organization. See particularly Debra P. Steger, "A Tribute to John Jackson," *Michigan Journal of International Law* 20 (Winter 1999), p. 165, and Joel P. Trachtman, "John Jackson and the Founding of the World Trade Organization: Empiricism, Theory , and Institutional Imagination," *Michigan Journal of International Law* 20 (Winter 1999), p. 175.

4. For the views of globalization critics, see John Gray, *False Dawn* (New York: New Press, 1999); William Greider, *One World, Ready or Not: The Manic Logic of Global Capitalism* (New York: Simon and Schuster, 1997).

Chapter Two

1. Under the unconditional approach to most favored nation policy, the benefits of bilateral trade negotiations were extended generally to all participating nations. The conditional approach provided for the

generalization of benefits to all countries making equivalent concessions of their own. For a recent history, see Eckes, *Opening America's Market,* pp. 90–93.

Chapter Three

1. *Washington Post,* May 5, 1997; *New York Times,* May 5, 1997; *Washington Post,* May 16, 1967.

2. See President Kennedy's comments upon signing the Trade Expansion Act, October 11, 1962, *Public Papers of the Presidents [John F. Kennedy] 1962* (Washington, D.C.: GPO, 1963), pp. 759–60.

3. Blumenthal soon became involved with trade issues, when he succeeded consultant Warren Christopher as cotton textile negotiator. Blumenthal negotiated a five-year cotton textile agreement that he says "was supposed to be the last cotton textile agreement ever negotiated."

4. Chairman Mills attracted media attention after police stopped his car near the Jefferson Memorial in Washington, D.C., on October 7, 1974. Argentine stripper Fanne Foxe (Annabel Battistella) jumped from his vehicle and leaped into the nearby Tidal Basin.

5. Myer Rashish, a former staff aide to the House Ways and Means Committee, worked on President Kennedy's White House staff.

6. McGeorge Bundy was special assistant to the President for national security affairs (1961–66). Carl Kaysen, an economist, was his deputy (1961–63).

7. Dale Hathaway, involved in agricultural negotiations during the Tokyo Round, told a Pro Trade Group meeting on March 28, 1989, that the U.S. and EC were at loggerheads over agricultural issues in the 1960s, 1970s, 1980s, and perhaps earlier: ". . . it was reported that when Lyndon Johnson was told that agricultural success or agreement was blocking the deal in the Kennedy Round of trade negotiations, he said, 'Cut a deal. Forget agriculture, et cetera.' And they did." "Pro Trade Group, the GATT: What's at Stake," March 28, 1989, Lexis-Nexis.

8. See U.S. Tariff Commission, *Trade Barriers,* inv. 332–66, 332–67, TC Publication 665, April 1974.

9. Memoranda from National Security File, box 52, Lyndon B. Johnson Library.

10. Ambassador Lang offered these remarks in May 1967, two months before the East Asian financial crisis began. Some rapidly emerging markets, like Indonesia, collapsed, raising questions about the viability of open-market solutions.

Chapter Four

1. The U.S. imposed a $10.50 per gallon excise tax on all distilled spirits produced in or imported into the United States. Prior to the Tokyo Round agreements, two methods were used to calculate the duty. Domestic production was taxed using the proof-gallon method based on both alcoholic content and volume. But bottled imports were taxed on the basis of volume alone, the so-called wine-gallon approach. Because such imports frequently contained less than 100-proof, this approach resulted in higher effective duty on bottled imported spirits. It thus provided the incentive to bottle imported spirits in the U.S. See U.S. House of Representatives Committee on Ways and Means, Trade Agreement Act of 1979, Report to Accompany H.R. 4537 (96th Cong., 1st sess., July 3, 1979), House Report No. 96-317, pp. 156-72.

2. "Information News Package for the Tokyo Round of the Multilateral Trade Negotiations," 1979, copy in Chief of Staff-Butler, box 2, Jimmy Carter Presidential Library.

INDEX